Smarter Budgets,
Smarter Schools

Smarter Budgets, Smarter Schools

How to Survive and Thrive in Tight Times

NATHAN LEVENSON

HARVARD EDUCATION PRESS
CAMBRIDGE, MASSACHUSETTS

Library of Congress Control Number 2011941942
Paperback ISBN 978-1-61250-138-3
Library Edition ISBN 978-1-61250-139-0

Published by Harvard Education Press,
an imprint of the Harvard Education Publishing Group

Harvard Education Press
8 Story Street
Cambridge, MA 02138

Cover Design: Sarah Henderson
The typefaces used in this book are Sabon and Frutiger.

*To my wife, Leslie,
and children, Alex, Aaron,
and Sarah, for all
the missed dinners
due to endless nighttime
budget meetings.*

Contents

1

The New Normal

OLD APPROACHES WON'T
WORK ANYMORE

As funding for education declines and student needs rise, public school systems can no longer rely on the strategies of the past. Four new overarching approaches must govern future budget deliberations.

"This is the tightest budget I have experienced in thirty years of school administration," said the superintendent. "We are long past cutting fat, we are cutting meat to the bone," a school board member added, and another concluded, more graphically, "It feels like we are cutting off our own arm, fat, flesh, and bone alike."

There is nothing surprising about this interaction given the funding shortfalls brought about by the great recession and the end of the funds from the American Recovery and Reinvestment Act of 2009 (ARRA). The surprise is that this conversation took place in 2005, the good old days, when this school system was wrestling with just a 3 percent *increase* in spending.

Historically, a tight school budget meant that the increase in spending didn't cover the rising cost of wages and benefits, nor the expanding services required for students learning English or with disabilities. Districts got more funds, just not enough more. The budget crisis of the next five to ten years will be different. Many districts will experience true cuts to total funding, compounded by escalating health, pension, and special education costs, putting enormous pressure on what's available for teaching and learning.

The well-tested strategies of reducing administrators, trimming supplies, turning down the heat, delaying maintenance, or forgoing a cost-of-living wage increase won't balance future budgets. Rather, new approaches, mind-sets, and tools will stock the budget survival kit of superintendents and school board members for years to come.

The situation isn't all bad news. Experience, research, and best practices can create a path to higher student achievement, despite lower spending. In every state, there are districts that outperform higher-spending systems with students from similar socioeconomic backgrounds. By studying what's worked elsewhere, by drawing on approaches used by nonprofits and the private sector, and by shifting our mind-set from the typical to the possible, students can weather this financial storm unscathed. If the current budget crunch forces districts to start planning from a blank slate, then students can actually benefit from the new approaches to K–12 education. Superintendents, school board members, education reformers, and anyone worried about educating our children in a time of declining resources will find practical, actionable advice and even a bit of hope in the pages that follow. I've also provided more than a few self-proclaimed "crazy ideas" to push the conversation outside the box.

Few gains come without pain and suffering, however. Just as Orbitz eased buying a plane ticket and ATMs lowered the cost of banking, travel agents and bank tellers were hurt. Since school budgets typically comprise 90 percent personnel expenses, smarter budgets can lead to smarter schools, but they will, unfortunately, have a human cost as well as a financial one.

Education has long suffered from clever ideas that turned out to be not that clever. Whole language, classroom technology, and zillions of hours of professional development, for example, haven't always delivered on their lofty promises. *Smarter Budgets, Smarter Schools* draws upon proven, successful practices that really have worked in the complex setting of twenty-first-century school districts. The ideas are drawn from many sources. As a business executive turned superintendent, I applied firsthand many of these approaches to the tight budgets of the Arlington, Massachusetts, public schools. Despite declining resources, our district significantly expanded our elementary reading program, enhanced our science and technology offerings, provided travel opportunities to the far corners of the world, upgraded college counseling services, made more parents of children with special needs happier, and enacted lots of other good things not typically associated with declining resources. Equally important, more kids learned more. The number of students reading below grade level dropped by 65 percent, English language learners (ELLs) surpassed the state target set for the district by more than 40 percent, and the special education achievement gap narrowed by two-thirds at the high school level over four years.

Beyond personal experiences, I have traveled the country looking for other districts that figured out how to do more with less. Over the last few years, my work as managing director of the District Management Council—a consulting, research, and technology company with a network of the most forward-thinking school districts in the country—has also provided a unique look under the hood of more than fifty districts from coast to coast, ranging from small suburban districts with just a few thousand students to large urban districts with more than 150,000 students.

For the bold or desperate, I also offer a few "crazy ideas" that are untested, but might dramatically bend the cost curve. These ruminations are clearly marked, so there's no chance that you'll confuse the uncommon but proven with the potentially crazy.

What is a good budget? It's a basic question for a book on school finance, but as a country we haven't answered this question for the new era of fiscal fragility. In the more flush past, a good budget was one that ensured that kids learned, all the existing staff returned, the books and maps stayed current, schools had enough secretaries so principals didn't do their own filing, facilities were gleaming modern buildings, four computers lived in every room, and a few interesting electives like ceramics, Mandarin, or afterschool robotics were offered. It also assumed that teachers got cost-of-living raises, earned pay bumps for taking college classes, and could stay in their same school each year. And finally, albeit a bit grudgingly, it meant generous health and pension benefits for all. By their actions, most communities thought any budget that could do all this was a good budget.

Few, if any, districts can imagine this scenario returning anytime soon. So a good budget today is one that at least reflects funding realities. Perhaps a good budget for the years to come will also be one in which struggling students reach grade level, high school graduates are ready for college or work, the arts and athletics are part of every school day, and school employees are treated as fairly as how most taxpayers are treated at their workplaces. This isn't the same definition as in the past, but it is possible.

If school districts are going to thrive in tight economic times, then four guiding principles will lead the way—and getting comfortable with the seemingly odd is the most important.

Embrace "Crazy" Ideas, Like Sushi at the 7-11

Public schools have, in my experience, tended to cling to a set of operating principles and assumptions, and anything that strays too far from the norm is deemed wild and impossible. But it's time and place, not cold logic, that define what's outlandish and what's not. In the 1960s, when I was a child, no one ate raw fish, or even knew anyone who did— at least not in suburban Massachusetts. That was crazy! Unbeknownst to me, it was commonplace in Tokyo. Move ahead forty years, and my children devour sushi and think it is as normal as a cheeseburger. Raw fish is still raw fish, but it has passed from odd to being available at the convenience store down the street.

Nearly every budget planning meeting I have attended—and I've been to enough for a lifetime—has assumed that the school day will begin and end as it always has, that kids all go to school about 180 days, and that each classroom will have a teacher (or two) in the front and about twenty-five students at desks. This arrangement costs, on average, about $12,000–$13,000 per student each year. Unfortunately, the cost to maintain this structure grows 5–6 percent each year. Many districts won't be able to afford this anymore. Many will miss its passing, but it hasn't always met the needs of students, and something that looks very different may very well replace and surpass it.

Make Better-Informed Decisions: The Angel Is in the Details

The current system of educating students, staffing schools, and building thoughtful budgets needn't be scrapped completely anytime soon, but it will benefit greatly from decisions based on much more detailed information than is typically available in most districts.

Budget documents often run to a hundred pages or more, but despite their heft, they often lack the most basic information for those charged with managing the budget. Most superintendents know off the top of their heads how many first-grade teachers work in the district, and many instantly know how many art teachers and librarians there are as well. In district after district, virtually none know how many special education teachers or speech and language therapists they employ. Most striking, a majority of the districts struggle to know the head count of special education staff, for example, even when they have their budgets in front of them. Those same superintendents know that high school math teachers have five classes a day, but almost none knows (or can find out) how many hours a week special education or ELL staff spend actually teaching children versus being in meetings.

Management guru Peter Drucker said, "What gets measured gets managed," and this is also true in schools. When the details are collected, analyzed, and shared, opportunities to reduce costs by a third or more jump from the page.

Duh! Spend Only on What Works

It's happened to most of us. We are thirsty, but the four quarters we just shoved into the vending machine didn't release the can of soda or give back our dollar. After pondering and debating with ourselves, we decide to try one more quarter—maybe pushed in a bit harder and straighter. No one would come back every day for 180 days and deposit a dollar into the broken vending machine without ever getting a Coke. Many school districts, however, are unknowingly doing something similar.

The kindest cut of all is to stop a program, practice, or pedagogy that isn't helping students learn. Not only does it reduce the budget, but it also removes the student from an ineffective situation. It's hard to know what's working or not, but the last twenty years have seen a steady rise in teachers, technology, curriculum, software, and support staff, with only modest gains in NAEP (National Assessment of Educational Progress) scores, the nation's report card. Ineffective practices and programs lead to costly remediation and intervention. Certainly, some schools and districts have made big gains in student achievement. If all districts weeded out what doesn't work and expanded what does, then students and the budget would both benefit.

Align Interests—a Cheeseburger Is Good, but Not for the Cow

Alfred Hitchcock's classic movie *Lifeboat* opens with the passengers of a sinking ship eagerly helping survivors into the one remaining lifeboat. Camaraderie and joy over their shared good fortune at reaching safety begin to dissipate as food and water run short. The analogy may seem melodramatic, but the anguish that superintendents, school boards, and others experience over cutting dedicated staff can make it feel like an equally desperate situation.

Principals worry about the children (and staff) in their building. The special education director worries about children with disabilities (and their teachers), and the math department head . . . well, the pattern is clear. These parochial interests make it very difficult to find efficiencies and to thoughtfully discuss options. Smarter budgets will take teamwork, and teamwork requires putting the good of the whole ahead of individual concerns.

Many a good idea has been held hostage to the desire to protect the current staff. Online learning is seldom embraced for fear of cutting teaching positions, and therefore, many online learning programs are staffed with full-time teachers, thus raising, not lowering, the cost of the class. When more cost-effective special education service-delivery models have been adopted by school districts, many roll them out only as fast as staff turnover. In other words, as teachers leave, the new plan is implemented for the new hires, thus protecting existing staff.

These four guiding principles—embracing "crazy ideas," analyzing details to make informed decisions, spending on what works, and aligning interests—can allow school districts to look at budgets in a new way. If the focus stays firmly on students, and the odd becomes commonplace, then this era of economic scarcity needn't be a step backward for America's children. I worry, however, that districts will simply do less of the same, rather than more of something different. I hope this book will provide district leaders and others big ideas and small details to ensure that tight finances don't hurt our children's future. As a veteran of years of budget battles, I know this will not be easy or painless, and good people will be displaced, but the alternative just isn't acceptable. The ideas in the following chapters will guide district leaders and school boards through a new, challenging reality. Good luck—I hope it helps.

If you have more good ideas to share, please e-mail them to me at ideas@SmarterBudgets.com. On my website at www.SmarterBudgets.com, readers will also find a number of interactive tools to help simplify some of the class-size and staffing calculations in this book.

2

Trading Down

DOING DIFFERENT, NOT LESS

The term budget cutting *implies doing less for students. Trading down embraces doing the same for students, but at less expense. Districts can shift to new cost-effective strategies for art, music, PE, library, IT support, assistant principals, and other roles.*

The worst part of balancing a shrinking budget is creating the *cut list*—the programs or services that a district won't provide next year. This is becoming an annual ritual in many districts. When done well, the cut-list discussion centers on the relative merits of one use of funds versus another. Many an elementary school has cut art to save reading. Nurses and social workers have been trimmed to save math and English. Wrestling with the trade-offs is important, but it is not as child centered as considering providing a service or support *differently*, rather than *not at all*. Often, it seems like the only choice is to do something the same or do less of it. There is a third way. It is called *trading down*. As the full force of the funding shortfall hits, districts must embrace new ways to serve students, even if they seem very odd right now.

Some of these alternatives aren't as good as the original, but they are better than cutting it completely. One way of trading down is to substitute less skilled staff for certified teachers. There is actually a long history of doing this (but maybe not in the right places). Many districts use paraprofessionals (also known as aides or teaching assistants) instead of reading teachers for reading help, and noncertified tutors also provide academic support in many districts.

Move to Lower-Cost Staff

If districts move less mission-critical functions to less skilled staff, and supplement with careful hiring, good supervision, and some professional development, they can still serve students adequately at a much lower cost. A few examples:

- One district replaced certified librarians with library paraprofessionals. No one would say this was a step forward, but it allowed each school to add a certified reading teacher. The district reasoned that it was better to have the certified teacher focus on reading instruction rather than the also important, but less critical, library skills.
- A suburban district replaced some IT support staff members—the people who install software, troubleshoot printers, and help teachers use technology—with tech-savvy moms working part-time. This wasn't ideal, but many had engineering degrees, and even though the pay was about half that of the regular staff, they took the jobs for the flexibility, the desire to work in their local schools, and as a first step back into the job market.

Trading down can also provide new services even during times of deep budget cuts. As a superintendent, I struggled with the harsh reality that while the budget was shrinking, the mental health needs of our students were increasing. Parents and staff rightly told me we needed social workers, mental health professionals, and drug and alcohol counselors. They added that these troubled students often brought their challenges home, so we needed family counseling too! The few guidance counselors we had at the secondary level spent much of their day dealing with scheduling, college applications, and discipline. We didn't have any counselors in the elementary schools. Special education individualized education plans (IEPs) consumed what few counseling resources we had, yet many of our neediest students weren't covered by an IEP.

It seemed unlikely that we could afford to add social workers; the idea of providing counseling to parents—when we couldn't even provide it to students—was unthinkable, and the school board had clearly established that "protecting the classroom" came before mental health. This seemed like a perfect case of something being better than nothing.

At almost no cost to the district, we were able to provide fourteen full-time equivalents (FTEs) of graduate-student social workers who were required to work half-time for a year as part of their master's degree program. They were supervised and guided every week by a very experienced therapist. These interns handled many of the mild cases and freed up our staff to focus on the more complex needs. Most principals found their help and support to be of great value. It wasn't perfect, but it beat the alternative—no help at all.

Look with Fresh Eyes

Human nature makes it hard to look at new ways to meet an old need. The old way is comfortable, and in many cases is working just fine as is. Why fix what isn't broken? Because many districts simply can't afford to maintain the old ways of educating students. So, something must change.

Familiarity can lead to complacency. I have noticed in life that the longer I experience something, the more normal it seems. I remember walking into a very nice house that was clearly well cared for. That being said, I was surprised that the paint was peeling off the molding, the rug in the den was stained, and one couch was worn threadbare. More glaring was that the guest bathroom had a cracked mirror and a broken towel bar. Most surprising of all, the house was mine, the bathroom the one I used every day for years, and the den my childhood hangout. I had been away at college for just nine months but on return saw, for the first time, what had been all around me for years.

I experienced similar "clear sight" revelations the first time I went to hire teachers. I had known since my days in elementary school that districts had only two levels of staff in a building, teachers and paraprofessionals. The "aha" came when I realized that no matter what the task, we hired teachers for one set of needs and paraprofessionals for another set. Each group had a uniform salary schedule, workday, and work year.

When I shared with my leadership team my shock that we had essentially just two levels of staff in a school, they were surprised at my surprise. It seemed completely normal to them. In fact, they couldn't think of any alternatives. To make my point, I shared with them the hierarchy of staffing in a doctor's office.

Thirty years ago, a typical doctor's office also had two levels of staff—doctors and nurses. Over time, however, the roles and pay structure have become much more specialized. Nurses no longer welcome patients; the clerical staff does this. LPNs take your blood pressure and basic stats; a physician's assistant may take your medical history or even diagnose a simple problem like an earache. The doctor is reserved for work requiring a very high level of skill and training. Today, there are at least seven levels of medical help where two seemed fine at one point (see table 2.1).

All this stratification was driven by the need to do more with less, without sacrificing quality of care. This parallels the challenge many school districts face, and so can some of the solutions. I know that some of these changes will seem odd or even undesirable, but I caution that it may be because you've been working in the current structure for so long that, as with my childhood home, it is hard to see what needs updating.

Overcome Moral Outrage

The shift from certified librarians to paraprofessionals exemplifies many of the pros and cons of trading down. The first challenge is to overcome

Table 2.1

Medical staffing

Then	Now
Doctor	Doctor
Nurse	Physician assistant (PA)
	Registered nurse (RN)
	Licensed practical nurse (LPN)
	Certified nursing aide (CNA)
	Medical assistant
	Secretary

moral outrage. Simply starting the conversation can lead to a lot of hurt feelings. I wasn't surprised that, when I raised the topic in Arlington, the librarians were upset; that was very understandable. The principals and my leadership cabinet were equally outraged. "These are great, loyal people; they are professionals!" my administrators declared. I agreed: they were good, caring people, but so were the untenured classroom teachers who were likely to get cut to balance next year's budget. Two things made the pushback more intense. First, this was a small, well-defined group. Everyone knew exactly who would be impacted, whereas simply cutting teachers across the board impacted "nameless" people. The actual people affected by an across-the-board cut wouldn't be named for months. The other contributing factor is that efforts to trade down can seem like an attack on the subject or profession. "Why do you hate librarians?" I was asked again and again.

For the record, I love libraries and books, and championed reading efforts in many districts. It is important to position this discussion as "because we must" rather than "because we want to." Certainly, I would have preferred to keep certified librarians in each school, but we didn't have the funds to continue with the status quo; something had to change.

Dispel Misinformation

Misinformation, even more than hurt feelings, tends to cloud the conversation of serving students differently. Within a day of announcing that I wanted to *study* the impact of shifting from certified librarians to library paraprofessionals at the elementary schools, the community was inundated by "information" such as:

- Librarians are required by law.
- Librarians are required by union contract.
- Librarians are critical to our reading program.
- Librarians teach skills required by the state curriculum guidelines.
- Librarians teach critical twenty-first-century skills, such as separating fact from fiction on the Internet and using the Internet safely.
- Librarians are overwhelmed with all they currently do, and no one would take the job at a paraprofessional's pay.

- And the most persuasive, pull-at-the-heartstrings counterargument: the children love the library, so they will lose their love for reading.

This list of reasons why we can't (not *shouldn't*, but *can't*) surfaced in less than a day and grew every day thereafter, or so it seems. If the information was true, then I shouldn't or couldn't go forward. It's funny, I seldom had heard how important the one period a week of library was before we put on the table the idea of changing it. Fortunately, we had four months before we needed to make a decision.

Start Early and Research Deeply

Because I had started rethinking how we provide library services and skills far in advance of budget season, my team and I had ample time to get the facts. We formed a study committee to get to the truth. It included some librarians, but the majority were people more able to be objective. We interviewed each librarian at length. We got their weekly schedules, we observed library classes, and we had short focus groups with students as well. Finally, we collected lots of documents—or at least tried to. In short, we gathered facts and gained a clear picture of what library was all about.

What we learned changed the discussion:

- A certified librarian was required at the high school for accreditation purposes, but *not* required at the elementary or middle school level.
- The union contract did *not* require certified librarians.
- Librarians were *not* part of our reading program. They probably should have been, but they had not attended a reading department meeting in decades, they didn't have or use any of the reading curriculum materials, and they didn't provide reading services. This surprised many, and it started to open the minds of some. A change in library staff might not be as detrimental as first suspected.
- The librarians in most of the elementary schools, it turns out, did *not* actually teach a whole lot. We asked all the librarians for

their curriculum and lesson plans. We received only their weekly schedule. When we asked for a list of what they'd taught in the last thirty days (content, themes, or assignments), we received nothing from some and a one-hundred-page printout of the state literacy framework from others. In fact, not a single curriculum document or plan existed. This surprised us all. Our observations of many library periods painted a picture of either silent reading or reading aloud as a whole class. It was reading, but it wasn't *teaching* reading. Most surprising was that kids often brought their books from their classroom to the library. As part of our core reading program, we had invested heavily in leveled classroom libraries, and students almost always were in the middle of a book and didn't want to start a new one for just forty-five minutes.

- I was pleased to learn that each librarian did discuss safe Internet surfing and how to evaluate online sources. These were the twenty-first-century skills we prioritized. I was disappointed to learn, however, that this discussion took place over only *a handful of periods a year*, and just for the older grades.

- Being a school librarian in Arlington was a nice job. Since each school, regardless of size, had a full-time librarian, many librarians taught only one-half or three-quarters of a full teaching schedule. They organized the library with what time remained. Since there was no curriculum or lessons, there was no planning or grading. One by-product of this light workload was that librarians seldom left the district, so many were at the top of the teacher's pay scale, which rewarded longevity.

Taken together, the research findings created a picture that differed greatly from the panic that surrounded the initial discussions. It was important that the research was detailed and methodical, and blended hard facts, observations, and extensive interviews with the librarians themselves.

Embrace Lower-Skilled Options for the Greater Good

The leadership team decided that the best way to improve literacy and balance a shrinking budget was to shift from certified librarians to library aides and use the savings to (1) add certified reading teachers, (2) develop a library curriculum, (3) expand in-class libraries, (4) provide extra support to the principal, and (5) help maintain small class sizes by reducing the number of teachers to be laid off.

We created a new level of staff: library paraprofessionals. Their hours differed from other paraprofessionals in that they were paid to attend regularly scheduled districtwide library instruction planning meetings. The qualifications were also different from other paraprofessionals in the district, requiring a passion for literacy, a love of books, and in many cases, interest in being a teacher.

The savings were significant. As table 2.2 indicates, a small district saved nearly $340,000 a year and freed up eighty periods a week of extra support for the principals, and few students noticed the difference.

The principals also realized that since each full-time staff member was expected to teach twenty-five periods a week, and our schools needed only twelve to twenty periods of library a week based on the number of classrooms in each building, the unscheduled time would be directed by the principal as needed throughout the school. The fact that the principals would gain some extra help, and the commitment to enhancing literacy elsewhere, got the principals on board. When we decided to fund a summer library curriculum planning effort for a week each year out of the savings, their support turned to strong advocacy.

Table 2.2

Trading down: Librarian example

	Before	*After*
Staffing type	Certified teacher	Library paraprofessional
Number of elementary schools	7	7
Number of librarians	7	7
Salary plus benefits	$525,000	$175,000
Curriculum investment	$0	$10,000
Net savings or available for redeployment		**$340,000**
Free periods for assignment by principal	0	80

When fully implemented, the paraprofessional-led library program was good, but not great. Some of the staff members hired were strong; others, not so much. The turnover was higher, and more supervision was required. Despite the downside, the money we saved was redirected to higher-impact uses. Most importantly, from the students' perspectives, virtually nothing changed. Library was still once a week, and they read, were read to, and learned about Internet browsing.

The lesson from this example is not "swap librarian aides for librarians." That would be a misread of the story. Rather, the takeaway here is to deeply understand the skills and work required of a role and then match the skills and pay accordingly in an effort to concentrate limited funds where they have the greatest impact on student achievement.

Evaluate Existing Positions Based on Skills Required

The core components of the trading-down strategy are to:

- Ask "Who does what?" in a very detailed way
- Honestly assess the required skills
- Ask whether someone else can do the work well, but at a lower cost

The role of assistant principal (AP) can often benefit from such an analysis. Some APs evaluate teachers, manage the special education staff, hire faculty, and run the daily operations of large complex schools. For these roles, the APs need to be administrators, and the job is appropriately matched to the skills and compensation.

On the other end of the spectrum, not all APs do mostly high-level work. In one low-spending, small district, the superintendent was bemoaning the fact that the district couldn't afford an elementary curriculum director. Money was tight, so new positions were out of the question. He had tried repeatedly to increase the budget to add this important position, but to no avail.

In desperation, the superintendent decided to look at the roles of all administrators in the district to see if responsibilities could be shifted around to fill this gap. I was tasked to help. When I tried to set up an interview with an elementary AP of a large school, the principal nearly blocked my way. "I couldn't live without my AP," she told me, "I would likely leave if you cut her position." Forewarned, I conducted the interview. For the first fifteen minutes, I learned how indispensable the role was, including conducting teacher evaluations, hiring, being second in command, and the like. As I pressed for details, the AP snapped and said, "Do you want to know what I told my mother, when she asked what I do?" A little stunned, I said, "Sure." This former star teacher recounted her day. It began with bus duty, ensuring that there was no rough play before school; she then covered classrooms when teachers had parent meetings, oversaw lunch, ordered supplies, and was back on bus duty at the end of the day. Certain seasonal jobs like the start-of-the-year scheduling and end-of-year testing were a bit more demanding. Nearly in tears, she said, "I'm an overpaid recess monitor."

She had been hired as AP because she was a master teacher of math, and the school needed to focus on math instruction. Her day had become full of necessary but lower-level work, and no time was available for teacher development, hence the superintendent's desire to hire a central office, elementary curriculum person. The AP's job wasn't fulfilling, and it wasn't a good use of limited resources, either. I also understood why the principal valued the role so much. There was no one else available to deal with buses, lunch, or the other tasks. If she lost the AP, these tasks would land on her plate instead.

In many districts, APs are paid much more than teachers. In this district at the time, the salary was about $75,000 for the AP versus about $50,000 for the average teacher. After a detailed study of the actual work assigned to the AP, the superintendent and I determined that the role could be split into three parts: (1) little-kid oversight such as buses, lunch, and recess, (2) seasonal tasks, and (3) teacher training.

By breaking down the work into pieces, assigning the more mundane parts to lower-paid staff, and creating a few stipends for the seasonal tasks, the district was able to free up enough money for a full-time math coach or a half-time curriculum administrator. Table 2.3 details how to stretch $75,000 by taking a detailed look at roles and needed skills.

The principal who originally feared losing an AP appreciated that all the bus, lunch, and recess work didn't fall back on her, and the district gained more teaching and learning horsepower.

Table 2.3

Splitting and restructuring the assistant principal role

	Before	*After*
Assistant principal	$75,000	$0
Bus monitor		$10,000
Recess monitor		$10,000
Scheduling stipend		$2,500
Testing stipend		$2,500
Math coach		$50,000
Total	**$75,000**	**$75,000**

Understand the Philosophical Obstacles of Trading Down

The discussion of trading down also raises many philosophical considerations. The example of bringing in tech-savvy moms to help with IT is a great case in point. The school board thought it a prudent decision to halve the cost of basic IT support by creating a new tier of noncertified staffing. Over the next few years, the IT staff did a good job of maintaining the equipment, helping teachers, and basic troubleshooting. The new staff also seemed to like their jobs. Turnover was low, and their attitudes were great. The glass seemed half full.

For the superintendent, however, the glass was half empty. He didn't like the situation one bit. While he agreed that the quality of work was good—very good, in fact—the whole situation seemed wrong. He thought the IT staff should be certified and on the teachers' contract and pay scale. Anything less was unfair, unprofessional, and maybe even a form of exploitation.

A few years later, at the constant urging of the superintendent, the positions were switched to certified staff. The superintendent promptly hired some of the current staff (who had become certified in anticipation of losing their jobs otherwise) and gave them a 50 percent raise. As the years passed and they moved up the salary scale, their pay, including benefits, nearly tripled. Nothing changed for students, but the budget was in a deeper hole.

Looking back, the superintendent told me he was proud that he had righted this wrong. His feelings illustrate that over time, in many districts the two-level system of teachers or paraprofessionals has become deeply embedded, with anything less than a teacher deemed undesirable. Addressing the philosophical component of creating multiple levels and types of staffing is every bit as important (and hard) as the technical details.

Ask Whether All Subjects Require Equal Skill and Pay

The examples of trading down in library, IT, and even assistant principals are very district dependent. They might make sense only after a detailed review of the situation in each district. The idea, however, could be applied more universally.

While the question is certainly uncommon under the "old normal," new realities may force districts to confront it more broadly: when is a certified teacher absolutely required, especially in noncore areas like art, music, or PE? Believing that these subjects are very important components of a well-rounded education isn't the same as believing that *only* a certified teacher can provide quality instruction (notwithstanding state and union rules).

Consider Noncertified, Noncore Teachers

Necessity seems to be the mother of hiring noncertified teachers as well as of invention. I first saw trading down in noncore subjects put to the test when a high school PE teacher suddenly left school midyear. The superintendent knew he needed to fill the position quickly. While the search was getting under way, the super had an idea during his twice-a-week aerobics class at a nearby health club. He had just finished an energetic workout led by an outgoing, engaging instructor. He approached the trainer and asked, "Do you like kids, and what do they pay you?" She did like kids, and she earned less than half of what a PE teacher earns. She was also very knowledgeable about health, nutrition, a wide range of sports, and was CPR trained. Within days, the district subcontracted PE services to the health club instructor.

The reaction in the district was vocal and mixed. The students were very pleased. The classes were "more relevant" and the dialogue "very real," according to their feedback. Others thought this devalued the role and importance of physical activity and sent a bad message. The superintendent countered with the argument that this was exactly what most town residents wanted and received when they paid for a health club membership. Had they ever asked to see the teaching certificate of their personal trainer or aerobics instructor? Lastly, he reminded the critics that nearly all of the district's athletic coaches had no certification or formal training, but they had been trusted to lead the students in varsity sports. The following year, the role was filled with a "real" PE teacher, and the line item restored to its previous level.

A few years later, as I was looking at a large budget gap, I remembered the story and wondered what positions might not require a certified teacher. Since the school board was considering cutting elementary art completely, we investigated alternatives to outright elimination. A few options emerged, including volunteer parents who had artistic ability, a subcontractor to provide art instruction, or a partnership with a local art museum. The museum already provided afterschool children's art classes, which were taught by professional, long-time artists. The museum could likely provide staffing to cover all of the district's needs. Since it was a nonprofit, it just wanted to cover its direct costs, which might have saved more than half the cost of our own staff. The investigation of this option showed how deeply many are wed to the notion that only a certified teacher can teach our children.

I checked references, and the afterschool art classes seemed to be of high quality. The museum was also very committed to developing a curriculum that dovetailed with our social studies program—a goal we had long desired but never delivered on. Many principals, teachers, and parents, however, expressed concern that this was "watering down" our program and commitment to the whole child. It amazed me that hiring professional artists, partnering with an art museum, and revising the curriculum to add meaning and cross-departmental collaboration could be viewed as inferior to our current program. Because there was so little support, we moved on to other options to balance the budget.

We were unable to see a win-win because it looked different from what we had grown accustomed to. We didn't change art, but we did increase class size, reduce electives, and cut elsewhere. This was all the more disappointing, because the district had two living examples of something similar. Both art teachers at the high school were professional artists. One sold in galleries around the world, and was even given months off during the school year to further his career. The high school art program was always oversubscribed. I had assumed the success of the program stemmed from the teachers' talent and passion, but it seemed that others thought it was their teaching certificates that made all the difference.

Let the Marketplace Set Some Wages

As school districts struggle with declining budgets, an overarching question is whether we can afford to pay all teachers the same even if free-market wages for some roles are likely lower. This is not an anti-union stance, because nearly all union contracts, except for teachers', acknowledge different pay scales for different roles within the organization. General Motors has dozens of levels of workers in its union contract, including many levels for its white-collar engineers covered by union contracts. It is more a question of a uniform pay scale. Through the years, I have led or participated in many dozens of budget planning meetings, and they often start with an exercise to define the core functions of the district. Typically, it is expressed as concentric circles, with reading in the center, core subjects in the second ring, noncore subjects in the third, and so on.

In nearly every case, school boards and district leaders place noncore subjects like art, music, PE, and library in the outer rings. They are definitely important, but not the *most* critical. When forced to balance a budget, we often see this prioritization in effect. Art or PE may be cut back or eliminated to save the core from cuts. Rather than cut these valuable classes, however, we have a number of opportunities to provide 100 percent of the instruction at much lower costs. The possibility exists because in some cases, free-market wages are likely lower than current contract pay scales. In noneconomic speak, this means there are pools of quality instructors who would be willing to work for less, maybe much less, than what some districts currently pay. Some possibilities are listed in table 2.4.

Table 2.4

Possible alternatives to certified teaching staff

Traditional	New approach?
PE teacher	Athletic club instructor
Art teacher	Artists or art museum employees
Music teacher	Professional musicians and singers
Drama teacher	Community theater producer
Librarian	Supervised paraprofessionals
Technology support	Students
Registered nurse	LPN or paramedics
Social worker	Local nonprofit counseling agency
Speech and language therapist	Certified speech assistant

Paradoxically, in many districts I have studied, noncore teachers actually earn more than core teachers, have smaller class sizes, and carry smaller teaching loads. How can this be, if these very same school boards place them in an outer ring of importance? Two factors contribute to this misalignment: longevity and whole numbers.

All teachers are paid the same in a given district, but not really. They are paid per the same schedule, but actual pay is based heavily on years of teaching experience. The longer you have been a teacher, the more you earn (up to a limit). In many districts I have worked with, the noncore teachers tended to stay longer than core teachers, thus they sometimes earn up to 25 percent more on average than core-subject teachers in the same district. The other factor that raises the cost of noncore teaching is that often an individual school has just one or two teachers in a given noncore subject, but it may need only three-quarters or one and a half FTE. Often, the district rounds up to have a full-time person. Taken together, these two factors can raise the cost of providing noncore instruction to 50 percent more per student than core classes. This adds further pressure to consider alternatives. There aren't many examples yet, but subcontracting noncore instruction or creating differentiated pay scales within the union contract in theory could yield significant savings, with little or no impact on the quality of services to students.

To put the possibility in perspective, if a district of five thousand students could provide quality noncore instruction at what might be "market wages," the savings would be about $3 million a year. This scales to $30 million for a larger district of fifty thousand students.

Before you dismiss the idea as too far from the norm, note that there has been a growing trend toward districts subcontracting academic support services. The two biggest examples are afterschool programs and remediation services through NCLB's SES (Supplemental Educational Services). BELL (Building Educated Leaders for Life), for example, has been hired to run afterschool programming for more than twelve thousand children, providing both enrichment and extensive academic instruction. In the areas of SES, the cadre of providers includes national for-profits like Edison Learning, which serves more than twenty-five thousand students with supplemental support, small businesses, public school collaboratives, and nonprofit organizations like Harlem Children's Zone. In the state of New York alone, over four hundred organizations provide academic instruction through the SES option. These two areas have one thing in common: they are new and expanded services. They didn't displace existing staff and programming, so it doesn't seem as odd to have a third party provide the instruction to our students.

Secretary of Education Arne Duncan declared that public education must learn to adapt to a new normal.[1] It seems that, by definition, this will require new staffing structures; otherwise, isn't it still the old normal? Breaking the paradigm of just two levels of staff and imagining nonteachers providing part of our children's education are likely to be part of the future. The good news is that in twenty years, it will look and feel normal. Most importantly, our children will continue to get a well-rounded, engaging education despite fewer financial resources.

No More School Nurses?

Few topics can strike a nerve faster than budgeting for school nurses. Their value and necessity are beyond question. The number of students with allergies, asthma, and serious medical conditions is rising. What is also beyond question is that each state has a very different idea of what is reasonable. In Massachusetts, one nurse per school (at least) is the widely adopted norm. Even small elementary schools of two hundred students often have full-time nurses, and larger schools may have one full-time and one part-time, or even two full-time people. Any discussion of reducing nursing staff quickly stops when someone shouts, "Children will die!" They really do shout this, often in the press.

I have visited nearly every state in the nation and am confident that parents outside of Massachusetts love their children just as much as we do in the Bay State. But, according to the National Association of School Nurses, the typical district nationwide staffs one nurse to every 1,151 students, compared to about one nurse to every 500 students in Massachusetts (based on informal research conducted when I was studying the topic as superintendent).[2] I have heard of some schools staffing one nurse to every two thousand students. In many parts of the country, it is common for one nurse to cover two or three elementary schools. In Massachusetts, this would often be unthinkable. Many schools in the state with just a few hundred students have full-time nurses.

This wide difference in staffing intrigued me. What is the right amount of staffing for nurses? After about nine months of research, I began to think this might be a case where doing things differently was a better avenue to pursue than looking at doing less. The research showed that the life of a school nurse is complex. Lots of routine scrapes and stomachaches, a bunch of paperwork, and on a fairly regular basis, something serious—an allergy attack, seizures, possible concussion, or worse. It seemed our RNs were overqualified for the Band-Aids and paperwork, but certainly needed for the more serious situations.

Similar to the assistant principal and librarian research, a study group looked in detail at the role of a school nurse in the district. Treating routine needs seemed very straightforward. In fact, if a minor incident happened at home, a parent or even an older sibling could handle the problem. This assessment was reinforced when we learned that, because substitute nurses were so hard to hire, the school secretary often covered for a nurse who was out sick.

I wondered and worried about what they did in other states that staffed far fewer nurses when a child had a seizure or other serious crisis. Turns out, they usually call 911. To my surprise, even though we had a full-time nurse, my district also called 911 almost every time there was a serious incident. The research indicated that our RNs were overqualified for much of what they did, and they felt they needed 911 support for the more complicated situations.

This seemed like a good opportunity to look for a different solution to meet a real need, especially since our nurses were mostly at the top of the pay scale due to their longevity in the district, earning nearly $80,000 with benefits. Being on the teacher's pay scale also meant that nurses worked a teacher's hours. This was not good for our students. The elementary schools wanted early-morning coverage because they had a lot of bruises and emotional meltdowns before the start of the official school day, and the high school wanted coverage during after-school sports. Neither was possible.

It turns out that we could get 911-quality support without calling 911. The research team discovered pediatric paramedics, one more link in the complex chain of medical personnel. These are the very people who come when we call 911. They are trained in childhood emergencies, and unlike a school RN, they can actually administer emergency medicine.

The really surprising part: they earn about half of what our school RNs earned. They expect to work fifty hours per week about fifty weeks per year, which is nearly twice the hours of a typical school nurse work year (six and a half hours a day for 180 days). What all this adds up to is that we could have full-time LPNs (a less skilled nurse) in every school starting an hour before school, plus our own pediatric paramedic circulating among schools via radio and on site for afterschool sports.

I assumed the school board would debate the mix of LPNs, pediatric paramedics, and maybe RNs or even secretaries. The case seemed strong—more coverage, higher skills, and savings of more than 50 percent. The board's first reaction was a simple "No, thanks." When I pushed, they said, "Actually, we hate it; it's dead on arrival (pun intended)." I dropped it. As our budget reality grew bleaker, and perhaps because of a stubborn streak, I brought it back to the school board one more time. Again, they said, "No, thanks; it just seems too weird."

3

Managing Benefit Costs

TAKING ADVANTAGE OF
EXISTING OPTIONS

*Instead of waiting for governors or Washington to rein in health
and pension costs, many districts have a number of options
available that don't require union approval or new legislation.*

As school budgets shrink, one line item continues to grow at double-
digit rates—health insurance costs. Although less visible and imme-
diate, pension costs are also absorbing a greater share of education
dollars. A recent study by the Massachusetts Business Alliance for Education showed that school districts in the state experienced health insurance increases averaging 13.6 percent a year from 2000 to 2007.
This amounted to $1 billion in additional premiums.[1] To put this in
perspective, state aid to schools increased by just $700 million during
the same period. Remember, these were the boom times before the great
recession, when states were increasing aid to schools. Benefit costs, unfortunately, are crowding out other educational spending.

I wish painless strategies existed for reining in health and other benefit costs, but there aren't many. Most private-sector organizations and

nonprofits have simply cut benefits or shifted more of the costs to their employees. Many school boards have tried to do the same, but with much less success at the bargaining table. This chapter provides strategies for reducing benefit costs that don't require union approval.

These strategies provide a route to lower costs, but not without real pain. Teachers, paraprofessionals, and other staff are significantly impacted, and this can't be sugarcoated. As resources shrink, the needs of adults and the needs of students will, at times, clash. Benefits are one such case. Most taxpayers have already experienced cutbacks in their work-life benefits, but that doesn't make it any less painful for educators.

If nothing changes, many districts will be forced to cut staff and reduce services for students as a result of ballooning health insurance and pension costs. Insurance rates, obviously, are high for all organizations, not just schools. IBM and United Way, for example, both struggle with double-digit premium hikes year after year. School districts, unlike the private sector or the nonprofit world, have a few additional hardships, however. In many districts, how much a teacher contributes to the cost of health insurance premiums and the design of the plan (co-pays, deductibles, and services covered) must be negotiated with the union.

Teacher health insurance costs can be dramatically more expensive compared to private-sector norms. The typical private-sector employer pays about $11,300 per employee for family coverage, after considering employee contributions.[2] But for the average school district in Wisconsin (a recent hotbed of benefit reform controversy), health insurance costs $20,052—nearly $9,000 more per teacher.[3] Some districts, especially in certain states like Texas and Florida, provide much less generous coverage, but it is not unheard of for teacher health insurance costs to top $25,000 after employee contributions.

Recently, a number of governors have stepped into the fray to try to change the system. In Wisconsin, for example, the governor passed a law requiring all teachers to pay a larger portion of their retirement and to limit collective bargaining of their health insurance premiums. Even in predominantly Democratic Massachusetts, the governor helped push through legislation that limits the ability of teachers and other municipal workers to bargain over health insurance by setting a ceiling on benefits based on a more cost-effective and flexible state-selected group of health plans.

Rather than wait for every statehouse, however, to help address the health insurance challenge, individual districts can take a number of smaller steps that don't require new laws or even new contracts. In my experience, two of the biggest differences between how the private sector and nonprofits manage health care costs compared to school districts is that they track health spending in more detail than school districts and are willing to work those details to their advantage.

Know Your Health Insurance Costs in Detail

It would be neither fair nor accurate to suggest that school districts don't worry about health costs; they worry a lot. Not all districts, however, feel they can do much about them. I empathize with the sense of inevitability. I have participated in a number of union negotiations, and nothing is more acrimonious or emotional than discussions of health insurance. In my negotiations, we mostly offset the few concessions we gain by approving larger raises to "buy" union agreement of the new plans.

Some districts have had greater success managing health costs away from the bargaining table. The first step is to know your costs in fine detail. This may seem obvious, but there are many reasons this isn't always the case. In some districts, especially in the northeast, health insurance costs aren't even listed on the school district budget at all. Because they are paid by the town budget, that's where they are listed. This doesn't mean that the schools are shielded from the impact of rising insurance costs. As rates rise, the town gives less money to the schools, but the direct linkage isn't made as obvious to school district budget developers.

I polled all the school board members in one such town during a budget development meeting. I asked, "How much do we spend, in total or per teacher, for health insurance?" As they flipped through their hundred-page budget briefing books, which included the cost of occupational therapy travel ($800) and elementary art supplies ($2,500), they could not find any reference to health insurance, even though the district spent over $10 million last year. It was listed in the town budget, not the school's. A few school board members mistakenly believed that because it was on the town side, the district budget was uninfluenced by these costs. In fact, the plan in front of them was to lay off teachers to cover a 12 percent rise in health insurance premiums.

Tackle Insurance Costs One Group at a Time

Most districts, including all independent school districts, do list health insurance on their budgets, but that doesn't guarantee sufficient detail. In every district budget I have reviewed (and I have read many), health insurance is a single, albeit large, line item. Why should this matter to anyone other than, perhaps, a CPA? Because tackling health care costs requires multiple strategies targeted to specific groups. If the line items align with the targeted groups, then the budget discussion tends to focus on each group separately. A single line item obscures the different avenues of attack. A common set of groups might include:

- Teachers
- Retired teachers
- Paraprofessionals
- Administrators
- Grant-funded staff
- Non-unionized staff
- Each union, such as maintenance, bus drivers, clerical, etc.

What defines each group is that its rules for health insurance *can* be different from the others. While many districts have just one set of rules, plans, and premiums for all employees, they don't have to—they just choose to. For example, in one district, principals and senior central office administrators had the same generous health plans as the teachers. This isn't surprising but for the fact that neither group had any bargaining rights. The district could unilaterally set rules for them. In fact, over time, the district moved its leadership to a plan more in line with the private sector, which saved money and set an example for future negotiations with teachers.

The desire for a single health plan can run deep and strong. Many HR departments much prefer a single plan for its ease of day-to day-management. Beyond simple logistics, I have often heard, "It's just not fair!" In an environment where all teachers get paid the same regardless of student achievement or subjects taught, it is natural that identical benefits would also feel right.

The pressure for uniformity is exemplified by the fight over health insurance for retired teachers. In one district, for example, retired teachers got the same health plan, co-pays, and contributions as active teachers. While there was an obligation to provide coverage, there was sweeping latitude to set the rates and rules. Retired teachers are not covered by or part of any union. There was near-unilateral authority to pick the plan and contributions for retired employees, subject to a set of minimums. Despite this freedom, both groups (retired and active teachers) got the same health plans. This pushed uniformity to the extreme because retired staff members were not required to switch to Medicare when they turned sixty-five because they wanted to stay on the "teachers" plan. Keep in mind that nearly 100 percent of nongovernment retirees, from corporate CEOs to doctors and most everyone else, use Medicare as their baseline insurance when they become eligible. Retirees could have been offered a supplement to make up any differences between Medicare and the active teacher options and still save $10,000 or more per employee. Despite mounting layoffs, this too seemed unequal, and thus undesirable. It is interesting to note that a state municipal reform bill passed a few years later mandated that all retirees move to Medicare when they become eligible.

Another benefit of creating health insurance line items by group is that it encourages a district to fully understand the specific rules that govern each group. I was working with one well-run, midsized school district and asked what rules governed health benefits for paraprofessionals. The answer came back, "Same as the teachers." Just to be sure, I asked to see both contracts so I could compare. "Oh, you won't find it in the contracts; we just always match." These small details give a district room to maneuver when it is pressed to find savings to avoid cutting staff or services.

Another midsized district learned that its contract called for providing health insurance to any staff member who worked half-time or more. This meant that when a full-time position was split into two half-time roles, the total salary stayed the same, but the health insurance costs doubled, adding more than $15,000 a year with no additional service to children. Armed with this understanding, the superintendent compiled a census of part-time staff. One hundred part-time positions existed. By reposting all these as fifty full-time positions, the district saved $750,000 in health insurance costs each year, without reducing a single minute of service to children.

Another district's contract worked differently. Its agreement called for providing benefits only if an employee worked more than 80 percent of the week. And the benefits were big. The total benefits package cost $40,000 for some grandfathered into past plans. Many paraprofessionals were paid about $20,000, so their benefits greatly exceeded their salary. The district dramatically reduced benefit costs by structuring many of the paraprofessional roles as four-day-per-week jobs or by having them start around 10:00 a.m. each day. This was limited to staff who could reasonably serve children with a reduced schedule. It wasn't right for everyone, but many worked in different schools each week or moved through multiple classes in the course of a day. The change was invisible to the children they helped.

Look at Fully Loaded Costs

Breaking out health costs into more detail by group is a start to greater visibility, and in turn, to cost management, but it is not sufficient. Creating *fully loaded costs* can also help foster better decision making. A fully loaded cost is simply adding all benefit costs to the salary of each FTE in the budget, rather than listing them separately. Without using fully loaded costs, it is very difficult to compare alternatives.

Thinking about paraprofessionals, for example, changes significantly depending on whether salaries or fully loaded costs are considered. A paraprofessional began as a low-cost alternative to a certified teacher. In many districts, they are paid $15–$20 an hour, which comes to about $15,000–$20,000 a year. To put all my cards on the table, I am not a

big fan of using paraprofessionals to provide academic support (more
on this in chapter 6), so I often ask, "Why don't you use more teachers
and fewer paraprofessionals?" and the answer is always, "The paraprofessionals cost so much less!" My follow-up question is always, "How
much less?" Typically, the response is along these lines, "A teacher
makes $60,000 and a paraprofessional makes $15,000, so we can get
four paraprofessionals for the price of one teacher." This is a big multiple, but it's not true in many districts.

Looking at the same situation on a fully loaded cost basis yields a
very different picture. From a benefits perspective, the teachers in many
districts are a mix of singles and families, while a disproportionate
number of the paraprofessionals are families. In many interviews I have
conducted, one of the primary reasons paraprofessionals seek the position is for family health insurance. This means that, on average, the cost
of insurance for a paraprofessional can be more than a teacher, given
the higher premium costs for family coverage. These are easy figures to
calculate for any given district.

As table 3.1 reveals, the theoretical school doesn't get four paraprofessionals for the cost of one teacher, but rather just a little over two. At

Table 3.1

Benefits shift the trade-off between certified teachers and paraprofessionals

Considering salary only

	Salary
Teacher	$60,000
Paraprofessional	$15,000
Multiple	4×

Considering fully loaded costs

	Salary	Benefits	Total
Teacher	$60,000	$10,000	$70,000
Paraprofessional	$15,000	$15,000	$30,000
Multiple			2.3×

this exchange rate, perhaps converting to more skilled teachers makes both academic and financial sense.

I have worked with a number of districts that became much more interested in shifting resources from reading tutors (a form of untrained paraprofessional) to certified reading teachers once they realized the real exchange rate when benefit costs were included.

Considering fully loaded costs can also help reframe how one thinks about teacher compensation in general. I learned, a bit to my dismay, that many of my younger teachers (and some veterans as well) had second jobs to help make ends meet. They would rush from school and work as tutors, waiters, or retail clerks. I saw the opportunity for a win-win.

Full-time teachers were expected to teach five periods a day. I proposed inviting any teachers who had the blessing of their department heads to teach a sixth class each day. In return, they would get paid extra—one-fifth of their salary extra. This meant that a teacher earning $50,000 for five classes would get $60,000 for six classes. This seemed fair to teachers and could be more desirable and lucrative than a second job. Beyond helping the family budget, this was also good for the school budget. For every five teachers who signed up for this option, the district could hire one fewer teacher and save the cost of benefits. While the union originally seemed favorable to the idea, in the end it never got enacted due to union objections.

I remember falling into the trap of not considering fully loaded costs myself. I had wanted to increase the office support for my elementary principals so that they would spend more time in classrooms observing and giving feedback to teachers. This was a key element of our improvement strategy and warranted the investment. Because I had seven elementary schools, this meant seven secretaries at $35,000 each for a total of about $250,000. This was a lot of money in a tight year, but I thought it an important and worthwhile investment

When I floated the idea, I got a lot of pushback about whether this support could be sustained. This was a fair question, and I started to think about the costs a few years from now. I didn't like what I found.

Each person would receive health insurance, there would be raises and steps in pay levels, and years from now we'd face retirement costs and sick-day buybacks. Five years from now, this support could cost more than $500,000 a year. I had scraped together the $250,000 needed, but it was unlikely that, as the fully loaded costs rose, these positions would remain. Rather than abandon the idea, I went back to the drawing board and looked for a different solution.

When I recast the position as an office paraprofessional rather than a clerical position, the pay dropped. I then limited the position to nineteen and a half hours a week (about four hours a day) so that these positions wouldn't include benefits. Because these weren't union positions, they didn't get automatic raises either. The first-year fully loaded cost would be about $80,000 in total versus more than $350,000. The role was a big boost for the principals as instructional leaders, and was affordable now and would be in the future.

I didn't feel good about crafting positions that fell outside the union contract and were just under the requirements for full benefits. My original plan did none of this. It was simple, but it wasn't ever going to happen. Only by carefully navigating the rules can a district find a way to balance the budget, make instructional leadership a reality, and help schools thrive in tight financial times.

Consider Outsourcing; Everyone Else Is

No conversation about benefits is complete without stepping into the political minefield of outsourcing. While the private and nonprofit worlds have grown accustomed to having a mix of employees and outsourced functions, many school districts have been slower to embrace the strategy.

Outsourcing is almost always detrimental to the current staff. Remember, I started this chapter with the warning that there are not many win-wins in this arena, unfortunately. In union environments, outsourcing is difficult. The difficulty, however, is mostly political rather than contractual or educational. Beyond the obvious downside to staff, outsourcing can be fine for students, and can help balance the budget without cutting programs. In the context of steep reductions in spending and the related cuts to services to children, it might be better than the alternative.

Thinking about fully loaded costs becomes critical when evaluating the financial benefits of outsourcing; this includes pension costs as well as other benefits. Depending on the plan in place, pension costs are also a ticking budget bomb for some districts. Forbes reports that nationwide teacher pensions are underfunded by nearly a trillion dollars.[4] The big unknown is who will pay for these future pension costs. While the answer doesn't have much impact on next year's budget, it certainly impacts the budget ten years from now. The hallmark of municipal pensions is that they guarantee a fixed amount of money—say, 80 percent of final salary—for life. The amount is often adjusted upward each year for inflation as well.

In some states, such as Massachusetts, educators while they are working make a large contribution to their future pensions, and the system is on relatively strong financial footings. In other states, current employee contributions cover only a small portion of expected future payments. In these situations, reducing the number of people covered by the municipal pension system will help future budgets. There is growing pressure for municipal and state entities to shore up underfunded pension funds so that they are able to pay future obligations. This means making payments to these pension funds from current-year operating budgets to cover future payments. This could be a greater drain on available resources than health insurance payments. This problem has already arrived in some states. Illinois, for example, had to quadruple its payments to its municipal pension fund to $4 billion a year to get reserves slightly healthier. This is $4 billion no longer available for current-year school budgets.

Opponents of outsourcing don't always consider fully loaded costs. I remember when my transportation director came to me with great excitement. He had run some numbers and concluded that we could hire more in-house staff and cut back on subcontractors. I was pleased that he was looking to increase efficiency and applauded his initiative. There was only one catch. He hadn't included the cost of health insurance, pensions, vacation, or sick time, which collectively increased our costs by almost 50 percent. This story highlights the point that some administrators don't consider benefits as real costs. Benefits, however, can easily equal 100 percent of a paraprofessional's salary or 50 percent of a bus driver's. There are many reasons to consider outsourcing, and managing benefit costs is near the top of the list.

How significant should the savings be to consider outsourcing? Some feel that unless the savings are big, it is not worth it; others think that a tie goes to the runner, and outsourcing is prudent in a breakeven case. One difference in these analyses is future benefit costs. Public entities are often slower to change their benefit plans than the private sector, but many outsourced firms don't have the same limitations on changing benefits, so future costs are more likely constrained.

I have been surprised by how often the primary difference between the cost of district employees and outsourced ones is the size of the benefits package. In a number of cases, the actual salaries of subcontracted food service workers, custodians, or speech and language therapists were nearly identical to the union wages, but the health insurance was much less costly, and instead of a municipal-funded pension, there was an employee-funded 401(k) retirement plan. In Wisconsin, for example, the average teacher receives 74.2 cents of benefits for every dollar of salary, while the typical private-sector employee receives just 24.3 cents of benefits for every dollar of salary.[5] For a teacher earning $60,000, this is an extra $30,000 in benefit costs compared to market levels.

Outsourcing functions like food service, custodial, maintenance, and even special education staff is often fraught with politics and ideology. Some see it as union busting, and others see it as the free market at work. Each community will make its own decision on the philosophical pros and cons, but understanding the economics hopefully is a politically neutral endeavor.

When you compare the cost of outsourced services, the full outside cost is very clear: $1 million a year for food service, or $50 an hour for a speech and language therapist. The quoted price is fully loaded; there are no extras. The comparison costs—that is, the district's internal costs—are harder to calculate.

The fully loaded costs should include:

- Salary
- Health and other insurance
- Cost for coverage during vacation
- Estimated pension cost

Benefit costs can trump all other factors in the outsourcing analysis. A number of districts realized that paraprofessional benefits exceeded 50 percent of salary and were increasing by double digits each year. These districts opted to subcontract the positions to a local nonprofit special education collaborative.

There were a few surprises to these moves. First, the districts actually *raised* the hourly salary, which helped attract high-caliber candidates. Also, in one district, the paraprofessionals who were to be outsourced eventually matched the deal being offered by the subcontractor and their jobs stayed in-house, but without benefits.

Maintaining Quality with Subcontracted Services

In interviews with districts that have moved forward with subcontracting, many stressed that the financial savings were not the only driver or the greatest benefit. Beyond the philosophical objection to outsourcing, a common pushback is that the quality of services will decline. "Contractors aren't employees of the district, so they won't care as much about our schools and our kids." Based on the stories I have heard from districts that subcontract services, this disappointment happens sometimes, but not that often. There are a few reasons that the quality remains high. First, because making the decision to outsource is such a high-profile change, the district does a great deal of reference checking, and poor-quality providers are screened out.

Also, because most subcontractors are hired for a few years, providers know they must deliver high-quality services or they won't be renewed. Thus, they have a much stronger incentive than do staff members with guarantees of lifetime employment. One CFO explained that outsourcing custodial services was financially almost breakeven, but the new provider could clean at night when the building was empty, whereas district employees earned overtime for working past 4:00 p.m., so they cleaned while classes were in session. Flexibility was the edge, and the classrooms were clean either way, but instruction wasn't disturbed.

The same district also outsourced food service for one simple reason. The district's food tasted lousy, and kids wouldn't eat it. Despite years of the district trying to improve its offering, students repeatedly chose not to buy lunch. The outsourced supplier had well-tested menus and adjusted the choices based on buying patterns. In a short time, the number of students buying lunch rose dramatically.

Perhaps one of the boldest uses of subcontracting took place in a mid-sized district that had a chronically underperforming alternative high school. For years, student achievement scores were low and dropout rates high, despite the district's repeated efforts to redesign, restructure, and revamp. The district subcontracted the school's management to a private company with expertise and a proven track record of success with this difficult population, students who struggle in a typical large high school setting. The company, in turn, hired new staff members who believed in its approach and philosophy. The decision was cost neutral and very beneficial for students.

The most convincing reason that new vendors will provide quality services is that they can specifically screen and select staff based on the current indicators of quality. The key word here is *current*. In districts with low turnover, many of the staff members in a given department or role were hired twenty years ago, often for a different purpose than current circumstances demand.

Kindergarten aides were expected to help foster socialization twenty years ago, but they're recruited to help teach reading today. Kitchen staff members who are used to fried food and frozen vegetables might be less comfortable with designing and managing a salad bar and raising the nutritional value of lunch that kids want to eat. While this isn't always the case, I have seen some compelling real-world tests. A number of outsourcing districts offered current employees the chance to be the first to apply for their old positions. Often, many didn't have even the most basic requirements for the new posting, such as a bachelor's degree or job-related training. It speaks to how much some roles have changed when a district chooses to hire back only a small percentage of its current staff, given the opportunity.

Overcoming the "Us Versus Them" Mentality

Subcontracting is often viewed as a choice between "our people" (district employees) and "them" (outside subcontractors). Just below the surface, there is often an unstated feeling that "our people" are good, caring, and part of the team, and the contractors aren't. I have certainly seen many contractors work in isolation from district staff and become a silo unto themselves. I have wondered whether this scenario was one of their choosing or forced on them, but in either case it is not the best situation. When Arlington first subcontracted social work services to the graduate interns, I saw the walls being erected. If there was a scheduling problem, the principal wanted to know what "they" were going to do about it. When a social worker had a problem, the principal nicely said, "Not my problem; go see your boss." As the social worker slunk away, she mused to herself, *Don't I work for you when I'm in the school?*

The following year, we revamped how we interacted with the sub-contracted staff. The principals met the social workers before school began, invited them to the start of school orientation, and made sure their schedules allowed them to attend faculty meetings. Additionally, the principals met on a regular basis with the subcontracted social worker's supervisors. I also assigned a district administrator the responsibility of ensuring that the social workers became integrated into the district's and schools' daily life. In time, some schools even started inviting the social workers to staff birthday celebrations, the true sign of acceptance in the school community.

All this interaction led to a much deeper understanding of our sub-contractors. They were, in fact, shifting from a nameless vendor to a true partner. Turns out, the vendor wasn't a mean company; it was a nonprofit organization that provided counseling to troubled children and their families on a pay-as-you-can basis. The subcontractors were smart, caring people. To the amazement of some in the district, the social workers cared about our students as much as we did. With the walls torn down, some really great things started to happen. Students who saw the social workers during the school day could get extra counseling after school from the agency. Because the agency also had relationships with the families of many of our most troubled students, we could coordinate family counseling, which happened outside the school day, with the student support provided during the day.

This was a remarkably broad and deep continuum of services, all at nearly no cost to the district. That's right—there is a form of subcontracting in which the services are free, or nearly so. Partnerships with nonprofits and private pay providers can be formed and leveraged at no cost to the district.

Building and Nurturing No-Cost Partnerships

Buoyed by the success of working closely with outsiders, we embarked on expanding the concept of no-cost partners. In time, we had drug and alcohol counselors, rage management experts, and behavior specialists all on our team, but not on our payroll or in our budget. We created partnerships with nonprofit organizations and invited them into our schools. For example, we had up to four "outsiders" attend the high school's weekly "kids in need" planning meeting. This allowed a very high level of integration of community and school services, sharing of ideas, and coordinated support. In a hundred years, we would never have been able to create such a strong safety net on our own.

Subcontracting Noncore Instruction

Outsourcing is also a way, perhaps the easiest way, to take advantage of some of the ideas raised in chapter 2, especially the strategy of shifting some noncore instruction to noncertified staff. Subcontracting these services will likely make it easy to not run afoul of union work rules or state certification laws.

The idea of shifting some certified teaching roles to noncertified teachers will probably be quickly dismissed as odd, wrong, or just crazy. It is certainly a stretch from the norm, but districts are trying to cope with a new normal of significantly reduced funding, rising costs, greater needs, and a heightened desire to raise achievement. The savings from shifting noncore staff to noncertified professionals through outsourcing may be too big to ignore. As table 3.2 reveals, the opportunity can be large—up to $3 million for a midsized suburban district, and up to $30 million for a fifty-thousand-student urban district.

Table 3.2

Savings impact from trading down noncore subject teachers (5,000-student enrollment example)

Traditional model

Subject	Number of teachers		Cost per teacher	Total salary and benefits
PE	14	Certified staff	$75,000	$1,050,000
Music/drama	13	Certified staff	$75,000	$975,000
Art	8	Certified staff	$75,000	$600,000
Library	8	Certified staff	$75,000	$600,000
Gifted	4	Certified staff	$75,000	$300,000
Secondary electives	11	Certified staff	$75,000	$825,000
Total	**58**	**Certified staff**		**$4,350,000**

Model of the future?

Subject	Number of teachers		Cost per teacher*	Total salary and benefits
PE	14	Athletic club staff	$20,000	$280,000
Music/drama	13	Professional musicians	$25,000	$325,000
Art	8	Art museum staff	$25,000	$200,000
Library	8	Paraprofessionals with supervision	$20,000	$160,000
Gifted	4	Paraprofessionals with online activities	$20,000	$80,000
Secondary electives	11	Subcontracted	$30,000	$330,000
Total	**58**			**$1,375,000**

*Remember, a full-time teaching schedule is one thousand hours a year, about half-time in the private sector.

Managing Contracts

Nothing comes without a downside, and subcontracting is no exception. The most common problem isn't poor quality, however, but rather poor management of the contract itself. Negotiating a contract is a skill, and anticipating future needs an art. Often, the contract design is left to the relevant department head, who isn't necessarily a skilled negotiator.

A common pitfall includes setting fees based on current needs, not actual needs. For example, one contract paid about $1.5 million a year for special education services. This was reasonable for the services required per the current IEPs. Over time, as enrollment dropped and fewer hours were written into IEPs, the contract remained at the original fixed fee (plus kickers for inflation). In the end, the district was unknowingly paying for 25 percent more hours of service than required, eliminating any savings.

The rising costs of health insurance and pensions are two sides of a vise, squeezing district budgets. As undesirable as it is to reduce benefits for staff or to outsource as a way of managing benefits, districts may not be able to write off the options available, if they are going to preserve or expand services and supports for students.

A CRAZY IDEA?

Insourcing to Unpaid Students and Parents

Some districts look to outside vendors to perform food service, custodial, or IT support because it is less expensive than using district personnel. What about looking *inside* for free labor?

On an exchange trip to Japan, an elementary school principal invited me to lunch, which, like lunch with principals around the world, means eating with the students. I thought it a nice gesture that children did the serving, but this wasn't just a show for guests. In Japan, students serve and clean up lunch—starting in kindergarten. As a result, they have one food service worker for every three or four we have in the United States. I started wondering, how far could a school embrace free labor?

Some schools already meet the IT troubleshooting needs with free staff sitting right in every classroom. Few parents these days haven't turned to their children for help with a computer challenge. A few high schools employ their students to run the computer help desk, maintain the servers, do basic repairs, and set up new equipment. Some structure it as independent study, work study, or even as a for-credit class.

As odd as free parent labor may seem, many parochial schools couldn't exist without it. Parents run afterschool programs, help in the office, and prepare the building for the opening of school.

Students and parents aren't the only place to look for no-cost workers. Teachers could help out, too. In the private sector, I have seen custodial costs cut in half by management simply asking employees to empty their own trash cans each day and sweep the floor in their areas each week. We all do this at home; couldn't we do it at work?

4

Raising Productivity

ENSURING MORE LEARNING
WITH LESS TEACHER EXPENSE

*Higher productivity—getting the same or more learning with
fewer staff members or fewer staff dollars—is the fastest route
to smarter budgets. Both conceptual frameworks and analytical
tools can help school districts thoughtfully reduce staffing costs
without harming students.*

Archimedes said, "Give me a lever long enough and a fulcrum on which
to place it, and I shall move the world." As districts strive to do more
with less, teacher productivity is the longest lever available. Increasing
teacher productivity means getting the same or more learning with fewer staff members or fewer staff dollars. The concept of teacher productivity might sound corporate or not child-centered. But don't worry: the
focus is squarely on helping students learn more.

Big gains are possible for many reasons. Teacher salaries are the lion's
share of any district's budget, often 60–65 percent of total spending.
Even a small change adds up to a lot. Over time, teacher costs have risen
much faster than enrollment. As new needs have emerged, districts have

added many more types of teachers, such as autism specialists, English language learner (ELL) teachers, or elementary Mandarin instructors. At the same time, benefits costs associated with each teacher have grown much faster than inflation. The National Center for Educational Statistics reports that the number of students served by each teacher in a district has decreased steadily from 26.9 to 15.5 over the last fifty years, indicating that the number of teachers has grown nearly twice as fast as the number of students. Figure 4.1 shows the steady, inexorable climb in teacher staffing over time. Figure 4.2 shows the decline in the number of students served by each teacher, on average.

Managing teacher productivity is not a new concept. Class size decisions are a good example. Every school district, every year, carefully manages the productivity of elementary classroom teachers. Targeting a class size of twenty versus twenty-five is a significant productivity decision, and answers the question of whether one teacher can effectively teach twenty or twenty-five students. In an elementary school of three hundred students, if district A has an average class size of twenty and district B has an average class size of twenty-five, then district B will need only twelve classroom teachers (three hundred students divided by

Figure 4.1

Number of elementary and secondary teachers in US public schools (in thousands)

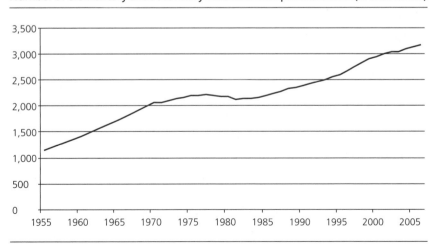

twenty-five students per class), which is three fewer teachers than school A. The teachers in district B have 25 percent greater productivity as a result of the class size decision.

So, a modest change in class size can shift the number of classroom teachers required by 25 percent—that's a lot of leverage for one decision. The savings are obvious, but at what cost to students? The critical question is whether the larger class size hurts or helps (yes, it might actually help) student learning. Whether you value smaller or larger classes, the good news is that there are many options available to districts to improve teacher productivity either way.

Understand the Unseen Cost of Smaller Classes

I never thought much about teacher productivity and class size until I was elected to my local school board. With my parent's hat on, it seemed plain obvious that smaller classes were better than bigger ones, ensuring more individual attention from the teacher and fewer disruptions. I was pleased that my district kept most elementary classes at around twenty students, and opted for eighteen or nineteen rather than

Figure 4.2

Students per teacher in US public schools

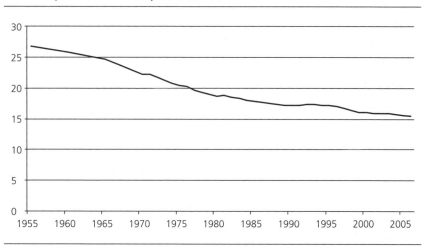

allowing the numbers to creep above twenty-two. As a district, we valued small classes and budgeted accordingly.

As parent-turned-board member, I asked, "How well do our students do?" It was a bit of a rhetorical question; we had great facilities, good teachers, and small classes. I was sure we were doing very well. Not so.

Despite our small classes, the district significantly underperformed against like communities, and teacher turnover was high. An eighteen-month study revealed that our teachers were basically left to themselves in their small classrooms; we offered no coaching, no mentoring, no formal curriculum, no common assessments, limited materials, no summer training, and not much professional development.

When I asked why we provided so little support to teachers, the answer was simple: "We can't afford it." With calculator in hand, I tallied what it would cost to add curriculum directors, mentors, summer institutes, and a district-run "university program" for new teachers; to increase professional development tenfold; and to stock the rooms with books and supplies. The bill came to $185,000 per school each year. In a fiscally conservative town, this kind of extra money seemed unattainable, yet it only required raising class size to twenty-two students, which was still small by most measures. To further make the case, I pointed out that nearly all of the like communities outperforming us had twenty-four or twenty-five children in each class but provided more support. After much debate, the district invested in comprehensive teacher support, and results skyrocketed. Students scoring advanced in math, for example, more than doubled after years of stagnation—rising to near the best in the state—from all the "extras" we could now afford.

Beyond this personal saga, the research on class size is unambiguous (although many still do not believe it):

- Most studies, including the well-respected Student Teacher Achievement Ratio (STAR) study conducted in Tennessee in the late 1980s, indicate that only very large reductions in class size—at least seven fewer students or a 32 percent drop—will impact student learning. Moreover, this gain is limited to the early grades and for students from impoverished backgrounds.[1]

- In my experience, almost no parents or teachers believe the research on class size, and not many administrators have either. At a recent superintendents' conference, a panel of veteran district leaders shared their advice for coping with tight budgets. Their message was simple: protect the classroom by protecting class size. Cut all else first.

Secretary of Education Arne Duncan said it well in his groundbreaking address on the new normal:

> Consider the debate around reducing class size. Up through third grade . . . a small class size of thirteen to seventeen students can boost achievement. Parents, like myself, understandably like smaller classes. We would like to have small class sizes for everyone—and it is good news that the size of classes in the US has steadily shrunk for decades. But in secondary schools, districts may be able to save money without hurting students, while allowing modest but smartly targeted increases in class size . . . It might be that districts would vary class size by the subject matter or the skill of the teacher, or that part-time staff could be leveraged to lower class size during critical reading blocks.[2]

All things equal, smaller class sizes are preferable, but at what cost? Supplemental reading programs, professional development, curriculum leadership, and the use of student data to drive instruction all have a greater impact on student learning and are relatively inexpensive compared to maintaining small class sizes. Despite their importance, these services are often cut, and cut deeply, during a downturn. These reductions save relatively little, but can dramatically reduce student learning. One district proposed eliminating the student data department and most curriculum leaders, halving professional development, and trimming reading intervention by a third—all to prevent average elementary class sizes from growing to twenty-one and a half students from twenty students. This was a popular decision, but not likely the best one for students.

The principal as instructional leader is often also sacrificed on the altar of small classes. Principals can drive improvement and support teachers only if they have time to visit classrooms, review data, and meet with staff. Yet many districts have quickly cut a school-based secretary or other help provided to the principal. This can eliminate half of the support system in the school, just to avoid adding one student to every other class. With the secretary gone, the administrative work shifts to the principal, and instructional leadership ends. With every potential cut to leadership support, ask yourself, "What will be added to a principal's plate? What will the principal stop doing?"

Not everyone will agree on what is an optimal class size, but I hope no one will disagree that it is important to manage class size strategically and thoughtfully.

Calculate the Financial Impact of Class Size Decisions

Knowledge is power. In my experience, most school leaders have a general sense that class size drives the budget, but they don't always have a firm number in mind. Adding one student per class can save more than 2.5 percent of total district spending (assuming teachers account for 65 percent of spending, and average class size moves from twenty-four to twenty-five students). Meanwhile, eliminating all professional development, mentoring, and coaching in a typical district might save just 1 percent of total spending.

When one urban district shared with its principals the impact of adding or removing one student in every general education class, the principals were certain a decimal was in the wrong place. Each additional student in a class equaled more than $10 million. Upon realizing the *opportunity cost* (what else they could do with even a portion of these funds), the principals nearly all reversed long-held convictions and advocated for closing a budget gap by slightly increasing class sizes while preserving or expanding other services for students.

What constitutes the right class size is a value judgment each district must make on its own, but knowing the true cost of class size choices can help inform its decision-making process. Table 4.1 helps put the range of savings in perspective for a typical school district at various levels of enrollment. A set of worksheets at the end of this chapter walks through the details of how to calculate the impact of changing class size in a given district. Electronic interactive templates are also available at www.SmarterBudgets.com.

Table 4.1

Annual financial impact from changing class size

	District enrollment: 5,000	District enrollment: 10,000	District enrollment: 50,000
Add one student per class	$650,000	$1,300,000	$6,500,000
Add two students per class	$1,300,000	$2,600,000	$13,000,000
Add three students per class	$1,900,000	$3,800,000	$19,000,000

Allocate Staff Based on Student Enrollment

Once a district has decided on target class sizes, implementing a methodical process of setting staff levels and assigning them to specific schools based on student enrollment and needs can dramatically reduce costs without impacting children. Many readers may want to skip ahead, thinking, *of course we do this already*, but in my experience, more can be done.

A district is *not* staffing to enrollment if it:

- Assigns one librarian, nurse, therapist, art teacher, or other staff member to each elementary school
- Has only full-time teachers at the high schools
- Doesn't move many elementary teachers between schools and grades each year
- Doesn't track the total teaching load of noncore teachers
- Doesn't regularly reassign teachers during the school year

The *concept* of staffing to enrollment is basic. The *politics* of staffing to enrollment is not! The idea is to hire and assign teachers based on how many students need to be served in each school, grade, or subject, and adjust each year as enrollment shifts. How to apply the practice varies by the type of role, as we'll discuss in the step-by-step process sections that follow.

A Process for Staffing Elementary Teachers

Many districts do an excellent job of staffing elementary classroom teachers to enrollment. A common budget-time ritual is calculating enrollment and determining how many teachers are needed at each grade at each school. Some districts, however, staff to *historic* enrollment. Student enrollment patterns change every year, but staff assignments may change less often. At a smallish elementary school, a drop of six students at a given grade level could reduce the need for a classroom at that grade level. Because teachers typically don't like to change grades or buildings, all the teachers at this grade level may just get smaller classes for a year.

For example, if the Kennedy School had five teachers at each grade last year, it faces great pressure to keep five teachers at each grade next year, even if enrollment has shifted. Some principals with declining enrollment fight to keep their current allotment of teachers as a badge of pride. Having fewer teachers somehow signals that they or their schools are less important than they used to be. Teachers, on the other hand, may not want to learn the curriculum of a new grade or move to a new school and learn a new culture. The reluctance of principals or teachers to shift around staff each year is understandable, but expensive. I have seen staffing to enrollment reduce total salary costs by 5 percent or more—that's $75,000 per school each year for a typical elementary campus of four hundred students.

The desire to anchor staff members to their schools can be so strong that one district maintained staffing patterns at schools even when enrollment shifted more than 20 percent over time. This created inequalities and greatly increased costs. Some second-grade classrooms had eighteen students while others had twenty-four—all because the number of second-graders living around each school had changed, but the number of second-grade teachers at each school had remained the same.

I understand why superintendents and school boards are reluctant to tackle this opportunity to do more with less. Few budget battles are more bruising than allocating teachers to elementary schools. Principals are pitted against each other, fighting for staff; some teachers rage at being forced out of "their" school; and parents are often dragged into the fight.

When I first tried to staff to enrollment as superintendent, some teachers enlisted the parents of each grade level that would be negatively impacted. The e-mails, phone calls, and pressure on the school board were relentless. A unique aspect of this kind of decision is that the people impacted are easily identified; they know exactly who they are, and thus are galvanized to react. The day wasn't long enough to meet with all the unhappy people, and I gave in (and learned). The stakeholders believed that maintaining staffing patterns was "normal" and what I proposed was radical. I needed to change expectations before I changed staffing patterns.

Develop Staffing Rules and Guidelines

My primary strategy was to jointly develop teacher assignment rules based on a series of what-if scenarios. For each school and grade, the district leadership team, months or years in advance, jointly decided what was reasonable at every possible level of enrollment. For example, we decided in advance that if we had sixty students, we'd require three teachers, but at forty-five students, we'd need only two teachers. We even decided, in advance, at what enrollment level a grade would automatically switch from three classrooms to two. Table 4.2 summarizes our thinking at one school. Notice how it goes beyond average class size targets, but fills in the decisions for *every* possible what-if scenario.

The detailed staffing rules showed all the possible combinations of enrollment, number of classrooms, and the resulting class size. By setting not only average class size targets, but also minimum and maximum class sizes, the answer to the question of how many fourth-grade teachers are needed becomes more automatic. In the case of two acceptable answers—for example, 104 students could be four or five classes—the leadership team decided in advance. This prethinking depoliticized the process and created the expectation that as enrollments changed, so would staffing.

A Process for Staffing Elementary Remediation and Support Staff

Few areas of school budgeting evoke more cries of "unfair" than the allocation of elementary support staff. Caring people of goodwill seem to have radically different definitions of what is equitable.

Table 4.2

Sample elementary staffing guidelines*

Target class size = 24
Minimum class size = 20
Maximum class size = 26

	Average class size				Average class size		
Enrollment	Three classes	Four classes	Five classes	Enrollment	Three classes	Four classes	Five classes
60	20	15	12	90	30	23	18
61	20	15	12	91	30	23	18
62	21	16	12	92	31	23	18
63	21	16	13	93	31	23	19
64	21	16	13	94	31	24	19
65	22	16	13	95	32	24	19
66	22	17	13	96	32	24	19
67	22	17	13	97	32	24	19
68	23	17	14	98	33	25	20
69	23	17	14	99	33	25	20
70	23	18	14	100	33	25	20
71	24	18	14	101	34	25	20
72	24	18	14	102	34	26	20
73	24	18	15	103	34	26	21
74	25	19	15	104	35	26	21
75	25	19	15	105	35	26	21
76	25	19	15	106	35	27	21
77	26	19	15	107	36	27	21
78	26	20	16	108	36	27	22
79	26	20	16	109	36	27	22
80	27	20	16	110	37	28	22
81	27	20	16	111	37	28	22
82	27	21	16	112	37	28	22
83	28	21	17	113	38	28	23
84	28	21	17	114	38	29	23
85	28	21	17	115	38	29	23
86	29	22	17	116	39	29	23
87	29	22	17	117	39	29	23
88	29	22	18	118	39	30	24
89	30	22	18	119	40	30	24
90	30	23	18	120	40	30	24

*Shaded area indicates actual classrooms per grade. An interactive version of this chart can be found at www.SmarterBudgets.com for making calculations based on a variety of target sizes.

If each elementary school gets one nurse, one reading teacher, and one speech therapist, for example, is this fair? When I first became superintendent, the one-per-school rule was set in stone and liked by many. Unfortunately, some elementary schools in the district had twice as many kids as others. Some had three times as many struggling readers as others. One per school seemed very unfair to me, especially to the children in larger schools who got fewer services because the staff was spread so thin. In my visits to school districts across the country, the one-per-school rule is common for one type of position or another.

Beyond issues of inequity, there is a financial downside as well. Let's say the Kennedy School and the King School each get one reading teacher, but based on the caseload Kennedy needs half a teacher and King needs one and a half teachers. The reading teacher and principal at King will rightfully lobby for more staff and may get a second reading teacher, even though there was extra capacity at Kennedy. Without staffing to need, the district will end up with three reading teachers when two would have been sufficient, or the students at King will be underserved.

As a nontraditional educator with a business and engineering background, I found it hard to understand how anyone—let alone a lot of smart, caring people—could embrace a rule that seemed bad for kids and the budget. After talking to hundreds of teachers and principals, I learned:

- Most teachers very much want to work in only one building, and for good reason. They shared horror stories of working in two schools but being part of neither. They weren't invited to faculty meetings or birthday celebrations at either. Mandatory meetings were set on days they were scheduled to be elsewhere. In short, they became second-class citizens in both places.
- Principals couldn't easily calculate the need in other schools and worried that whoever screamed loudest or had the most pull got more staff. At least one per school was a rule they could understand and wasn't subject to favoritism or other pressures.
- The central office didn't have the data needed to make more thoughtful allocations. The one-per-school rule was simple to administer.

A CRAZY IDEA?

Quadrupling Some Class Sizes

Most of the elementary schools I visit take for granted that noncore classes have the same class size as core classes. It's a given, they assume, that when the twenty-five kids in Mrs. Smith's class go to art, obviously the art class can't be any bigger than the twenty-five students from Mrs. Smith's class. If the students in Mrs. Jones's class are sent to art at the same time, however, then the school has increased class size and reduced staffing needs in art, without impacting the regular classroom. There are many variations on this theme, such as three classes split between two specials, or three classes at a single special.

At the secondary level, the same is true, except many classes in the arts have even smaller class sizes than math and English. Art rooms may hold only fifteen students, and musical instruction may be limited to ten students.

The initial reaction to the idea of very large class sizes for specials is typically 100 percent negative and along the lines of "these are young children, and the classes would be unmanageable." On the surface, this pushback makes sense, but in my travels I have seen:

- An elementary school band with eighty students and one teacher. This worked well for years without the district giving it a thought because band took place before school, and could only be scheduled as one session. When the very same district discussed moving band to during the school day, it determined that anything more than twenty-five students at a time would be overwhelming.
- One small school, which hated the idea of big classes, had for years combined four classes for the entire spring to rehearse for the school play and the school music performance. It had one teacher and one aide for eighty-five students and thought nothing of it because it was a special event.
- PE classes at many schools are capped at twenty-five students, but afterschool sports, led by the same PE teacher, have forty or fifty students per adult.

- In some low-spending districts, such as in Texas, elementary schools have had seventy-five students in a music or PE class for decades. The staff in these schools doesn't find it unreasonable, just normal.
- One suburban school, determined to create common planning time for teachers, brought together all the students in a given grade, nearly two hundred young children, each week for anti-bullying instruction and school culture development. Without intending to, the school created a special class of two hundred students with one leader and a few aides. The program was a success and continued without note. This was the same school that targeted eighteen to twenty students in a classroom, and thus had only eighteen to twenty students in art, library, PE, and music.
- Like other classes, music classes at one high school were limited to twenty-five students—except the school's award-winning chorus of eighty students, who practiced together each day. Unintentionally, the school had created an elective that had three times the typical number of students with just one teacher.

Why even consider an idea as crazy as quadrupling some noncore class sizes? Because it doesn't take one minute of music, art, or PE away from a single student. It doesn't increase core class size at all, and it reduces staffing requirements when budgets are so tight that some districts are taking away reading teachers, professional development, and other critical services. In some schools, they are even forced to reduce art, music, PE, and library!

The drawbacks are obvious, but the savings may not be. If a district of five thousand students doubled up classes for elementary specials and had large group art, music, and PE at the secondary level, it could save about $1.5 million a year. This scales to $15 million for a district of fifty thousand students. If a district added a paraprofessional to help manage the larger classes, 75 percent of the savings would still be possible. Classrooms may need to be modified, but in the long run, the cost of knocking down a wall to make a bigger room is small compared to the savings.

Based on some quick calculations, it appeared that in my district the one-per-school rule created very high workloads for about 20 percent of the staff involved and increased total staffing by 20 percent as well. Determined to relieve the overburdened staff, expand services where warranted, and reduce costs, we took the following steps:

1. *Create an easy-to-calculate measure of need for each service.* For reading teachers, need was the number of students scoring below benchmark on the Developmental Reading Assessment (DRA); and for special education therapists, it was the number of direct instruction hours with children per IEP.

2. *Assign less-than-full-time staff members to schools based on need.* If a school needed 0.8 teacher (i.e., someone working four days a week) or 1.2 teachers, that's what was assigned— no more, no less.

3. *Ensure a home base for each staff member.* Teachers who worked in more than one school had a designated primary school. They became part of the culture of that building.

This plan worked, and it had some interesting unintended consequences. Some teachers opted to work part-time rather than work in two buildings, and some principals combined two part-time roles into a single full-time position. Since the total staff allocation per school was set by the guidelines, the principals were empowered to mix and match as long as they didn't add cost to the district.

Create a New Definition of "Fair"

Figures 4.3 and 4.4 illustrate how different definitions of fairness play out. In this hypothetical district of ten elementary schools with ten reading teachers, one option would be to assign one reading teacher to each school (figure 4.3). This is simple and fair by some definitions. It is also very desirable for the ten reading teachers. Unfortunately, for the children in school number 2, this is not fair. There are more than twice as many struggling readers in school 2 as in school 5. Unavoidably, struggling

Figure 4.3

Assigning one reading teacher per school

	(1) Enrollment	(2) Students identified needing services	(3) Allocated staff (FTE)
School 1	350	35	1.0
School 2	375	45	1.0
School 3	285	25	1.0
School 4	425	40	1.0
School 5	275	20	1.0
School 6	450	25	1.0
School 7	380	35	1.0
School 8	290	36	1.0
School 9	350	20	1.0
School 10	290	40	1.0
Total	3,470	321	10.0

Students requiring reading support per reading teacher

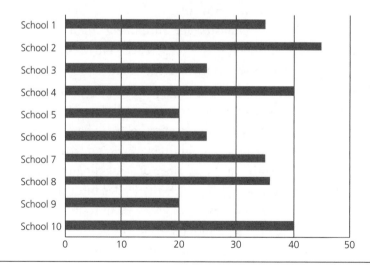

readers in school 2 will get less help than children in all other schools. Is this equitable? It would be easy, but disruptive, to allocate staff to each school based on the number of struggling readers. As calculated in column (3) of figure 4.4, school 2 requires 1.6 reading teachers, while school 5 can serve all its students with just 0.6 teachers. Figure 4.4 shows a much more student-centered distribution of staff than figure 4.3, but in both cases only ten reading teachers are needed.

It is easy for staffing and student need to get very out-of-whack. One large district had assigned academic support staff over the years based on a myriad of formulas. Each made perfect sense at the time. Reading teachers were assigned based on the one-per-school rule. Math support teachers were assigned to the schools with the lowest math scores, phonemic awareness specialists based on grant funding rules, special education teachers based on total school enrollment, extra reading teachers went to Title I schools, etc. As enrollment shifted and the years passed, these allocations stayed fairly rigid. Every year, most schools kept the staff positions it had the year before. The result was much inequity, from a system originally designed to be fair and thoughtful. Figure 4.5 indicates that some schools in this district had three times as many academic support teachers (adjusted for enrollment) than others. Title I status did not explain much of the difference. This resulted in vastly less remediation and intervention services in some schools versus others. In fact, which school a child attended determined whether that child would even have access to a given program at all.

Staffing to student need in my district helped create a new definition of fairness—one focused on children. When midyear assessments showed some sizable shifts in the number of struggling readers at some schools (up in a few, down elsewhere), the leadership team thought it fair that staff assignments be switched *midyear* in response to changes in student need. Given the high mobility rate of English language learners, we found that staffing patterns needed to be adjusted at the start of each marking period.

Figure 4.4

Allocating elementary staff between buildings

	(1) *Students identified needing services*	*(2)* *Percent total need*	*(3)* *Allocated staff (FTE)*
School 1	35	11%	1.0
School 2	45	14%	1.6
School 3	25	8%	0.8
School 4	40	12%	1.3
School 5	20	6%	0.6
School 6	25	8%	0.8
School 7	35	11%	1.0
School 8	36	11%	1.0
School 9	20	6%	0.6
School 10	40	12%	1.3
Total	321	100%	10.0

Students requiring reading support per reading teacher

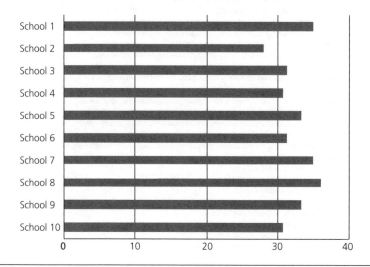

Figure 4.5

Students per remediation and intervention teacher

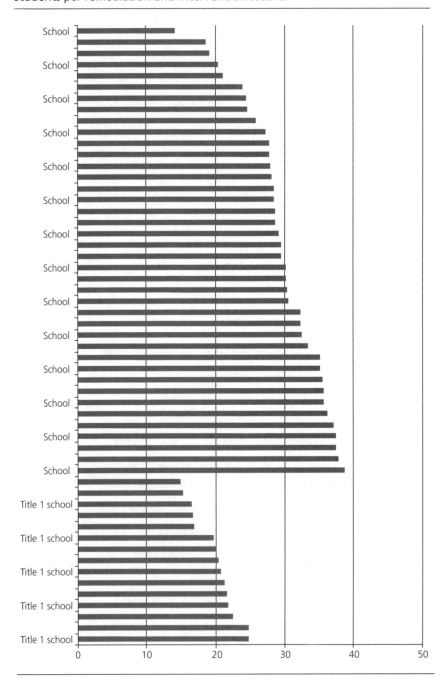

Align Resources with Current, Not Historic, Needs

It is hard to overstate the allure of staffing to historic need rather than actual need. When I first became superintendent, I did a quick study of ELL need versus staffing (and I mean *quick*—it took about an hour). I simply calculated ELL staff per ELL students in each school. It only takes a brief glance at figure 4.6 to see that schools 3, 4, and 5 had no ELL staff, and that the middle and high schools had only a handful of students assigned to each ELL student. Schools that historically had virtually no ELL students were omitted from the review.

I learned that most of our ELL students attended four elementary schools, and we had relatively few ELL students at the secondary level. I also learned that 60 percent of the ELL teachers were assigned at the secondary level, and two of the high-need elementary schools had zero ELL support.

Why such a misalignment of need and resources? I am fairly certain that the staff members were originally assigned based on where the ELL kids were, but they hadn't been reassigned for five or more years. Essentially, all ELL teachers created their own schedules and only wanted to

Figure 4.6

ELL students per ELL teacher

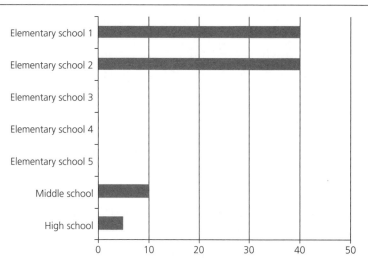

work in the building where their offices/classrooms were located. Each year, the principals of the two unserved schools clamored for hiring more ELL staff, assuming that the existing teachers were fully committed. Due to tight budgets, no new staff had been provided. In reality, we had much more staff than was needed; it was just in the wrong buildings. When I reassigned teachers based on student requirements, a grievance was filed for taking a teacher from "her" school. The district culture had deemed that ELL teachers were assigned to schools, not students. We did win the grievance, and a culture of reassigning staff, even midyear, developed. Best of all, the students started to excel. Over the next three years, ELL students surpassed the growth and performance targets set for the district by the state by more than 40 percent.

A Process for Staffing Elementary Specialists

One type of need is very easy to calculate but can run counter to the culture in some districts. The students in each elementary classroom typically go to "specialists" (art, music, PE, and library) one or two periods a week. This implies that a school with twenty classrooms will need to cover twenty periods of art each week. Union contracts almost always state what constitutes a full teaching load, such as twenty-five periods a week. This is an easy need to calculate based on the following formula:

$$\text{Elementary specialist staffing need} = \frac{\text{(Number of classrooms)} \times \text{(Frequency of instruction)}}{\text{Number of periods in a full teaching load}}$$

Worksheet 3, at the end of this chapter, helps organize the information to calculate the staffing need for each type of specialist in an elementary school. While the math is straightforward, the results often play havoc with custom in some districts. Based on my visits to schools across the country, some districts automatically create "itinerant" positions that move between schools as needed, while others staff almost exclusively to an individual school. Both strategies seem to be long-held practices—not often questioned, just inherited from past practice.

A related practice is the use of full-time staff when the need is only part-time. In some districts, elementary specialists are almost exclusively full-time positions. In my district, we had nearly all full-time specialists staff in the elementary schools, assigned primarily to one building. While this seemed normal to those who grew up with the practice, it struck me as an extravagance that diverted needed resources from helping our students. Despite severe budget cuts in the years before my arrival, including the elimination of all reading teachers, virtually no elementary specialists were assigned a full teaching load. A school with twelve classrooms, requiring twelve periods of library, had a full-time librarian, despite this being only half a teaching load. A school needing twenty periods of music had staffing for twenty-five periods. Simply by staffing for the need, as calculated by the number of periods to be covered, the district saved 20 percent on the staff to provide elementary specials. While this did create staff shared by two schools or some part-time positions, it also allowed us to hire back reading teachers. Keep in mind, we didn't decrease a single period of art, music, library, or PE.

A Process for Staffing Secondary Core-Subject Teachers

The concept of staffing to enrollment applies equally well to the secondary grades as to the elementary grades, but it is a bit more complex in practice. Many middle schools have adopted the model of grade-level clusters. This means one math, one English, one science, and one social studies teacher all instruct the same group of students at one grade level. This adds pressure not to shift teachers between grades or buildings based on annual fluctuations in enrollment. There is a desire, rightfully so, to keep teams together. In high schools, it is more common that teachers are regularly expected to teach classes at different grade levels based on enrollment.

The logic of staffing to enrollment for secondary core-subject (math, English, science, social studies, and foreign language) teachers is similar to elementary classroom teachers, but the politics and data gathering is more difficult. The two guiding criteria are:

- How many periods a day constitute a full workday? This is spelled out in nearly all contracts, such as five classes a day.
- What is the target class size for each section? Some districts may set smaller target class sizes for remedial courses or larger targets for honors and AP.

If we assume a target class size of 25, with five classes a day, then a core-subject teacher can serve 125 students. If that same teacher were expected to teach two lower-level classes with a target class size of 20, plus three typical classes, then the teacher can teach just 115 students. While the number of students served will vary, each teacher will teach five sections a day.

With these guidelines in hand, it is easy to determine how much staff is needed to meet enrollment. Let's follow an example of a high school with 1,010 students taking math.

1. Determine the number of students that signed up for each level of class.

	Students enrolled
Remedial math courses	200
Regular math courses	600
Honors/AP math courses	210

2. Set a target class size for each level.

	Students enrolled	Target class size
Remedial math courses	220	20
Regular math courses	600	25
Honors/AP math courses	210	30

3. Calculate the number of sections of math required. Simply divide the number of students enrolled at each level by the target class size.

	Students enrolled	Target class size	Sections needed
Remedial math courses	220	20	11
Regular math courses	600	25	24
Honors/AP math courses	210	30	7
Total			42

4. Determine the number of staff members required to teach all the required sections. This figure is based on what constitutes a full teaching load per the teacher's contract.

Sections required	42
Sections taught per full-time teacher	5
Teachers required	8.4

Hire Part-Time Staff for Part-Time Needs

Based on the course enrollment data, it seems that 8.4 teachers are needed to teach math to all the students in this high school. But in my experience, it would not be uncommon for this school to have 9 or 10 math teachers, not 8.4.

Why the difference? The first reason is that many principals and department heads prefer full-time staff members, so they round up to nine. This decision alone costs the district $45,000 a year. I have had pretty good luck hiring part-time staff members, who might be parents with small children, retired teachers, one teacher split between two buildings, or a dual-certified person who can fill two part-time positions.

Combine Small Honors and AP Classes

Honors and AP courses pose the second problem for staffing to enrollment. In a world crying for college readiness and rigor, there is pressure to offer a full range of these courses. What should a school do if only six students want to take AP French or eight want to take AP computer science? The two most common solutions are to offer the classes at a very high per-pupil cost or to cancel the class due to low enrollment. For an alternative answer, we can look to small and rural schools that regularly struggle with wanting to provide classes for small numbers of students. They rely on combination classes—for example, AP French, French 4, and honors French 3 are all taught at the same time by one teacher. Students get differentiated assignments and work in small groups. This certainly complicates lesson planning, but it may be better than either of the common solutions. By necessity, one small K–12 district with just over a thousand students routinely combines up to three high-level classes into one period, and nearly all of its students still achieve top scores on AP exams.

The other challenge to AP and honors classes is self-imposed. Some districts keep these classes small, presumably to facilitate discussions. I hear all the time from school board members who fret about the high cost of AP, IB, and honors classes. After visiting many such classes, it seems reasonable to me that twenty-five to thirty highly motivated students can be in one class. In theory, AP and honors should be the most cost-effective classes in any school.

Find a Scheduling Guru

Third, computerized scheduling doesn't make this type of staffing calculation easy. Most high schools use a computer to schedule students, and when a student needs to be in both calculus and French 4 and only one class exists for each, and both are held at the same time, it is common to create an extra section of calculus, resulting in two smaller classes. This is good for kids, but the cost isn't always taken into account. The decision to add a section seems cost-free because the school already has nine or ten math teachers. My experience has been that schools seldom *hire* additional staff to work around a student's scheduling conflict, but they will *use* any "excess" capacity of their existing staff to do the same. In both cases, however, the cost to the district is the same; it just feels different.

It turns out that some people are a lot smarter than a computer. I have had the privilege of meeting members of a special fraternity—secondary school scheduling gurus. They have an uncanny ability to improve the computer's plan and "hand schedule" the students who are necessitating extra sections. These gurus are often teachers or assistant principals, and it is not uncommon that they freelance over the summer, helping three or four different districts. A few thousand dollars invested for a week of their time can save $100,000 in staffing at each school.

Unfortunately, this detailed student-need based approach isn't really the way many districts think about staffing, especially in small or midsized suburban districts. The alternative approach starts with the teachers they have, rather than the students' needs. If the math department has ten teachers, there is great pressure to keep all ten. Only when a math teacher retires or moves away is the question raised: "Do we need nine or ten staff members in the department?" Like a vegan objecting to eating anything with a face, district leaders can find it very hard to look into the face of a dedicated teacher and say that he or she is not needed just because enrollment has dropped or shifted. Secondary school departments can be like families, and this creates an incentive to develop a schedule that "needs" all ten teachers.

The foreign language department at one suburban high school is a telling example of a district's desire to maintain current staffing levels. Over the years, the number of students taking Latin had steadily climbed, and the number of students taking Spanish had dropped. One Latin teacher taught 160 students, while two Spanish teachers had only about 60 students each. The district needed more Latin teachers and fewer Spanish teachers. The superintendent proposed adding a half-time Latin teacher and cutting one Spanish teacher. Both the department head (a Latin teacher himself) and the principal opposed the change. It didn't seem fair to the Spanish teachers or the Spanish department, they explained.

This example may seem too small-scale to be relevant for a large urban district, but big districts are just a collection of dozens, scores, or hundreds of individual schools, and the same process often plays out in each building. In some urban districts, staffing by subject for each school is set at the central office, and can be slow to change with shifts in school enrollment or course selection. I have seen gradual 30 percent drops in enrollment in a school fail to trigger a decrease in staffing.

A sharp increase in enrollment is more likely to bring about the hiring of new staff than a reduction will bring about a cut. Taken together, these forces make staffing *downward-sticky*, meaning it is easier to go up than down. When class sizes increase, teachers are added faster than they are reduced when class sizes decrease.

Align School Schedules and Foster a Larger Sense of Community

Creating a culture that assigns teachers where they are needed can have a significant budget impact. Districts can take a few steps to make this easier. A simple first step is to have all schools of the same level use the same bell and rotation schedule. It seems an odd solution to a staffing problem, but it does make a big difference. For example, if the King School and the Kennedy School both needed a science teacher for two periods each day, one person could work in both schools—but only if the schools have similar daily schedules; otherwise, each school is likely to keep a full-time person. Despite the ease and power of common bell schedules, they are very rare in my travels.

Another step that would help is to create more of a sense of community across schools. Joint department meetings or professional learning communities (PLCs) that aren't limited to a single school could spark districtwide professional relationships, which would ease the sense of loss when a staff member has to change schools. Neither solution is a cure-all, but both can make an undesirable situation better.

Focus on the Needs of Students, Not Teachers

The biggest challenge to implementing such an analytical approach to staffing is that it places an emphasis on stretching limited resources to maximize the support of kids. It deemphasizes the impact on teachers. In some schools, job preservation and staffing stability seem to trump all else. I have sat in on countless discussions that go like this:

Department head: I know that the fifty teachers in my department teach only 85 students on average, and all the others teach about 115. That's not their fault. They don't deserve to be let go.

Superintendent: If they taught 115 students like everyone else, we could save about $1 million, which can be redeployed or fill the budget gap. It doesn't seem fair to the other teachers either.

Principal: I can solve this; we will add some more courses for them to teach, including supplemental help, so they will have fuller teaching loads.

Department head: Great solution! Everyone wins.

Superintendent: Come on, we are creating a need to keep the staff. We wouldn't add these classes otherwise, and it will just create small classes in other departments.

Principal: I'll make this work. Don't you like these teachers?

The desire to protect "good people" from being let go just because schools don't have a need for them runs extremely deep in the culture of many (maybe most) districts. It is understandable, and in many ways is a sign of caring leadership. In a time of declining resources, though, it may not be sustainable or fair to students. Two extreme examples follow.

One district eliminated health from the curriculum by combining it with PE, so all the health teachers were cut from the budget. The director of the health department, however, wasn't cut because of her long ties to the district. For years, she oversaw a department of zero staff.

I know one teacher whose entire career seemed to be an endless series of "acts of job-preserving kindness." She was the least senior teacher in an elective department, which had plummeting enrollment. While most teachers in the district taught 115 students, five periods a day, she taught 65 students spread over four periods a day. How did the district respond? First, it created an administrator position for this tiny department and promoted her. It made her a part-time supervisor and part-time teacher, giving her a raise and justifying a reduced teaching load. Now she was now officially full-time "busy," giving her reduced expectations for teaching kids. As the budget shrank and her class enrollments shrank even more, the school considered not replacing a retiring teacher in another elective in an effort to force more students into her elective by reducing student options. When this didn't fly, and enrollment in the department dropped to the point where two teachers would be let go, the beloved teacher was promoted to fill an opening as assistant principal. It was openly acknowledged that she wasn't the first choice, or even the third, but the district "needed" to help her. She struggled with the job, but many assumed she would retire in a few years with full benefits. She deserved this! When yet more budget cuts came, and the school board cut one of the assistant principal positions, it seemed her time had run out. Not so. The principal announced he was retiring, and she could be principal for a year until she was ready to retire. I'm sure some would say she was qualified, and she was certainly certified, but nearly all the conversations about these three promotions focused on her needs, not her skills.

The majority of the staff believed this underutilized teacher turned department head turned assistant principal turned principal was not the best candidate for her ever-expanding roles, but they understood and supported the logic of "protecting our own." Given such strong feelings, analytical tools alone are very inadequate. The real question is "how do you create a system or culture that allows staffing based on student needs?"

Chapter 9 provides more systemic ideas for creating a culture that embraces staffing to student needs.

A CRAZY IDEA?

How About One Hundred Students in a Class?

This chapter has pressed the point that class size has a big impact on the budget. Most class size discussions focus on whether twenty-two or twenty-six students is OK for elementary schools and whether thirty in high school would be out of control. What about one hundred students in a high school class?

I know the idea seems crazy, but nearly everyone who attends college will have some classes of one hundred students or more. Whether it is freshman calculus, Economics 101, or Intro to Biology, some college classes are huge. This is true at Harvard and state colleges alike. Could high school seniors take college-style classes? Would this prepare them for what comes next?

My own children's education is a telling example. When my older son took AP calculus, his class had nearly thirty students. Because of a highly effective teacher, he (and most of his peers) did very well on the AP exam. My younger son, attending a different school that prized small classes, had an AP class with half as many students, but nearly no one in the class did well on the exam. The point is simple: the teacher matters more than how many desks are in the room. The irony is that the students at my younger son's school will retake the same course in college in a class of one hundred students or more. A class of one hundred would, of course, require a different teaching style, small group discussions, and tutoring.

While a class of one hundred is radical, an AP class of forty just requires ten more desks. It also lowers the costs for this class by 25–50 percent, and could increase learning. In a world of unlimited funds and unlimited great teachers, there isn't a good reason to consider mega-classes. Given our real-world constraints, however, there are a few benefits that make the idea worth considering:

Improving college readiness. Nearly all college freshmen will have lecture hall–style classes, and they would benefit from experiencing this environment while still in high school.

Leveraging outstanding teachers. Outstanding, highly effective teachers are sometimes in short supply, especially in math and science. Large classes allow many more students to experience high-performing instructors. Some great teachers teach mostly small sections of honors and AP, working with no more than eighty students a year. Imagine if they worked with two hundred students each year.

Facilitating dramatic pay increases for teachers. When I first met the president of the Arlington teacher's union, he asked me, "Hey, Nate, what would you choose for your children? Option one—you pick the teacher, any teacher you want, but thirty kids in the class; or option two—a randomly assigned teacher with fifteen students?"

Since I believed that the teacher matters more than class size, I chose option one. The union head told me most everyone does. He wanted bigger classes *so that* the district could afford higher wages. A district can afford to pay a teacher who serves 180 students a day 50 percent more than a teacher who serves 120.

If they're structured thoughtfully, large AP and honors classes can be better than smaller ones. So what does class size have to do with teacher quality? Potentially, a lot. Large classes leverage great teachers, but large classes might also *attract* great teachers as well. Much has been made of the fact that teachers in many high-performing countries come from the top third of college grads, which is not the case in the United States. If a district moved its average class size from twenty-five students to thirty-five students, it could raise all teacher salaries by $30,000 with no net impact on the budget. If, by implementing a combination of online learning (see chapter 7) and college-style lectures, a district had every teacher oversee the education of 200 students rather than the current typical 125, the average secondary teacher could earn $120,000 a year and the top of the pay scale could be nearly $150,000, without the district raising the overall teacher salary budget. Could this attract and retain more top talent to teaching? I don't know, but it might be worth a try.

A Process for Staffing Secondary Noncore Teachers

Staffing to enrollment for noncore (art, music, PE, and other electives) secondary teachers is similar to doing so for math and English, but has a few quirks and pitfalls to avoid.

As with core-subject teachers, the idea is to calculate how many students want to take courses in a given department, divide this by the target class size, and adjust if the class meets less often than every day. For example, if a class meets every other day, one teacher can cover twice as many sections.

Despite the simplicity of the math, staffing in noncore secondary departments is often far from optimal. In the majority of schools I have studied—including large urban, upper-income suburban, and middle-class districts alike—noncore secondary classes often have smaller class sizes, on average, than core-subject classes. That's right: often, a PE class has fewer students than a math or English class. Despite its pervasiveness, this is seldom a conscious school board decision. There are a number of reasons for the mismatch:

Schools want to meet all students' first choices. Creating schedules, especially at the secondary level, is complex and full of trade-offs. Since many electives are offered just once or twice in the schedule, they might conflict with other infrequent offerings. This means some students can't get all their preferred courses. Say ceramics and French 4 are only offered during second period, so the school wants to add another section of ceramics. This is great if the school can afford it. The real cost to provide this flexibility for a single student to take his preferred elective is about $15,000, since the extra section consumes one-fifth of a teacher's day. It is unlikely, however, if this same student petitioned the school board to add a *new* elective for him alone, that the board would approve a $15,000 expenditure.

The teachers are fixed and the enrollment varies. In many schools, the staffing is fixed and students must adapt. For example, in my district, we had two art teachers at the high school and four family and consumer science (the modern name for cooking and child development, and the successor to Home Economics) teachers. Each year, the art classes were oversubscribed and family and consumer classes under-subscribed. This meant art classes were maxed out, and many students couldn't take art at all. Family and consumer science classes were small, even with the students who reluctantly signed up because they couldn't get into art. This is unfair to kids, but it's also expensive.

Failure to readjust staffing to student interest typically leads to overstaffing. In one study in a midsized district of about fifteen thousand students, noncore classes at the secondary level were over-staffed by 25 percent. This wasn't a plan—it just happened, unno-ticed, over time. This district had already cut the budget in the prior years, but hadn't touched this area.

Teachers prefer to work full-time at one school. When you do the math to determine staffing to enrollment, often the answer is 3.6 art teach-ers, or 2.4 technology teachers. As with elementary noncore teachers, the middle and high school counterparts like to work full-time and in one building. This means four art teachers and three technology teach-ers will be hired. Some may not have full teaching schedules; some might cover lunch duty. Often, three classes of twenty-five will be split into five sections of fifteen. Everyone looks busy, but the school is still overstaffed based on student needs. Sharing staff between two build-ings and hiring part-time positions allowed one district to save nearly $250,000 each year in staffing at a single middle school.

Noncore teachers have longevity and community ties. Although it is hard to generalize, in many schools I have studied, the noncore teachers have significant longevity (very low turnover), are more likely to live in town, and have strong parent relationships. These are the teachers who lead the art shows, music presentations, and drama productions—all activities with high parent engagement. It is very hard to tell these beloved stalwarts of the community, who have worked in the school for twenty-plus years, that their positions are being cut because the numbers don't add up.

Change the Schedule, Not the Teachers

Another route to higher productivity is to spend the same but get more. Many a district has wished for a longer school year or school day. Most industrialized nations provide more time in class, and many charter schools do as well. Traditional public schools have struggled to fund an expanded school calendar because the implicit understanding is that more instructional time will require more teacher work hours and thus more compensation in return. Rethinking the teachers' schedule, as well as the students', can provide more time on task without an increase in cost. What if all special education teachers and remediation support staff started work at 10 a.m. instead of 8 a.m.? This would create an additional two-hour block at the end of every day, but no extra staff is needed and no teacher works more hours than before. This provides a longer school day at no extra teacher cost and is a great example of increased productivity.

I'll admit that this chapter lays out a very structured approach to staffing that is at odds with many current practices. It may seem a bit cold, and it is. At some point, as budgets shrink further, districts will be cutting so deeply into services and support that this analytical approach to staffing and its deliberate focus on productivity will seem student centered. These tools are for coping with the new normal, which will not be easy or enjoyable.

End-of-Chapter Worksheets

Interactive electronic templates can be found at www.SmarterBudgets.com.

Calculating the Impact of Changing Class Size

Each district starts with a different set of circumstances, and there is great value in calculating the specific impact of changing class size in a particular district. Worksheets 1 and 2 will help guide a district through the math.

It is helpful to consider target class size by *grade level* across the district, rather than a single, districtwide figure. What is appropriate for kindergarten may not be the same as for high school. Grade-level detail allows for grade-level discussions. This is a point worth repeating. If we focus on districtwide or schoolwide averages, it is harder to have a thoughtful discussion separating kindergarten options from fifth-grade ones. When I suggested raising some elementary classes to twenty-five students, parents and teachers immediately imagined twenty-five kindergartners in one room, and balked loudly. When I stipulated that it would only be fifth-grade classes, many found the idea much more reasonable.

Managing a school district isn't easy, and neither is managing class size. The worksheets will give a close approximation, but the details are tricky. Since you can't have three and a half first-grade classes in a given school, just three or four, it isn't possible to simply select the desired average class size. Moreover, averages can be misleading.

A secondary math department might be OK with an average class size of twenty-five, but not if some sections have twenty students and others have thirty, even if the average is twenty-five. Finally, substantially separate special education classrooms or special classes like English language learning complicate the math. Despite the complexities, the cost of changing class size is knowable and worth knowing.

Worksheet 1

How much is saved by adding one student to an elementary classroom?

Grade	(1) Enrollment	(2) Current number of classrooms	(3) Average class size	(4) Add one student per classroom	(5) Required number of classrooms	(6) Savings
Example	1,000	45	22.2	23.2	43.0	$150,000
K						
1						
2						
3						
4						
5						
Total						

Worksheet 2

How much is saved by adding one student to a secondary-level (core subjects only) classroom?

Grade	(1) Enrollment	(2) Number of sections	(3) Average class size	(4) Add one student per section	(5) Required number of sections	(6) Savings
Example*	1,000	218	23.0	24.0	208.0	$150,000
6						
7						
8						
9						
10						
11						
12						
Total						

*Example assumes each student takes five periods of core subjects a day and each teacher teaches five periods a day.

For mathematical reasons, it is necessary to use separate formulas for elementary and secondary classes, because secondary class sizes change each period of the day, while elementary classes are full-day.

The process has seven steps:

1. Enter total enrollment districtwide for each grade. Exclude students in substantially separate or out-of-district programs.
2. Enter the current number of classrooms districtwide for each grade.
3. Divide column (1) by column (2) to calculate the average class size for each grade.
4. Add one student to the class size calculated in column (3). This is the new hypothetical class size.
5. Divide the enrollment in column (1) this time by the new average class size in column (4). This indicates the number of classrooms and teachers needed, in theory.
6. Subtract the new number of classrooms needed, column (5), from the existing number of classrooms in column (2), to determine how many fewer classrooms are needed.
7. Multiple the average teacher cost, including benefits, by the number of classrooms saved to calculate the financial impact of adding one student to each classroom.

The same process, of course, works for adding more than one student. The secondary level is similar, but you do the math per section rather than per classroom.

Calculating Staffing Needs for Elementary Specialists

This four-step process will help determine the staffing needs of each elementary school. It assumes the traditional approach of sending one regular education classroom at a time to a special.

Worksheet 3

Specialists	(1) Number of regular classrooms	(2) Periods/week for students	(3) Total sessions required	(4) FTE required
Example*	20	1	20	0.8
Art				
Music				
Library				
PE				

*Example assumes a contract requiring 25 periods per teacher per week.

Full-time teacher, per contract, teaches = ___ instructional periods/week

1. Enter in column (1) the number of regular education classrooms in the school. Do not include substantially separate special education classrooms if these students are included with general education peers for specials.
2. Enter in column (2) the frequency with which each special meets each week. For example, enter 1 if students get art once a week, or 2 if students get PE twice a week.
3. Multiply column (1) by column (2) to determine the total weekly periods to be staffed column (3).
4. Determine staffing needs by dividing the sessions required by how many sessions a full-time teacher is expected to teach in column (4).

5

Academic Return on Investment

SPENDING ONLY ON WHAT WORKS

No district knowingly spends limited resources on ineffective
programs, but it's hard to determine which efforts are driving
achievement. Academic return on investment is a mind-set and a
tool for identifying what works, where to invest more, and how
to reduce costs but not learning.

Duh! Who wants to spend money on what doesn't help kids learn? No
one. But how many superintendents and school boards know what actually works in their district? Not too many.

Two truisms help frame this discussion: (1) no one knowingly funds
strategies, efforts, or programs that they don't think will raise student
achievement; and (2) despite the massive infusion of spending into K–12
education over the last twenty years, nationwide achievement has been
mostly flat, making it apparent that much of the new efforts haven't
been all that effective. Since 1992, eighth-grade NAEP reading scores
barely budged in the face of heroic efforts and spending to increase student literacy, and have been virtually flat since 1998.[1]

In good times, the typical annual district budget discussion goes something like this: "We need funds for math coaches to help implement the new math program, and grant dollars to expand professional development in reading, and resources to start a dropout prevention program, and more staff to add paraprofessionals to help struggling students." In each case, the asker is certain these efforts will raise student achievement.

In bad financial times, the conversation sounds more like this: "Don't cut the math coaches," says the math director, "they are crucial to our efforts to raise scores in math." "Don't cut professional development; it's the lifeblood of improvement," says the director of curriculum and instruction, "and, clearly, taking money from students at risk of dropping out would be cruel." And on it goes.

This isn't just administrators protecting their staff—it also reflects a deep-seated belief that these efforts are important and effective. In the end, whoever can tell the most persuasive story will carry the day. Imagine, however, if before the budget conversation began, the director for data and assessment made the following short presentation:

- Students of teachers receiving support from math coaches gained three and a half months of more learning than students of teachers who did not get coaching. Additionally, in 87 percent of unannounced observations, teachers who received math coaching were observed implementing the program with fidelity.
- Students of teachers receiving reading professional development (PD) fared no better than students of staff who didn't receive the professional development. Moreover, only 15 percent of unannounced observations revealed the PD content being put into practice.
- Of the students entering the dropout prevention program, 75 percent of those with grade-level reading ability (but with significant social, emotional, and/or drug issues) graduated, while only 5 percent of students with significant learning and reading deficits eventually graduated.

After such a presentation, it is very likely that math coaches will stay (or expand), reading PD will be stopped (or changed), and the dropout program will remain in place for one type of students, but not all. The problem is, this kind of hard data is seldom available, so debates and passionate pleas become the norm.

Imagine if the presentation went on to share this statistic:

- Teachers who received twelve hours of coaching had similar results to those who had thirty-six hours of coaching support.

The district might cut back on coaching without fear of losing the benefits.

Measure Your Academic Return on Investment

In a world of declining resources and a burning desire to raise student achievement, it seems unreasonable to children and taxpayers not to subject budget and pedagogy to this kind of scrutiny, called *academic return on investment* (A-ROI) analysis. Cost effectiveness—along with its sister concept, A-ROI—is both a mind-set and a decision-making tool. In essence, it requires that districts formally evaluate all programs, efforts, and strategies by multiple measures, including effects on student learning, number of students served, and cost per student. A-ROI seeks to maximize achievement for the greatest number of students given available resources. Many superintendents and school boards apply this concept intuitively. There is great benefit, however, in doing it *explicitly*. The formula is straightforward:

$$\text{Academic return on investment} = \frac{(\text{Increase in student learning}) \times (\text{Number of students helped})}{\$ \text{ spent}}$$

While the formula for A-ROI is straightforward, there are three powerful concepts hiding within:

- Not all money spent to help kids learn is effective.
- Money spent should lead to positive student outcomes.
- Spending $1,000 to help a student is better than spending $2,000 for similar gains.

Nowhere in the formula, however, is it measured or considered that "we have always done x, y, and z," or that the head of ABC department "is really passionate about the program."

Return on Investment as a Guide for Nonprofits

Long a cornerstone of resource allocation decisions in the private sector, return on investment has now entered the social service sector. When the Bill and Melinda Gates Foundation was first launched, its founders asked themselves how they could help the most people, with the greatest impact on their lives, for each dollar spent. At the time, HIV-AIDS was the front-page concern, but the foundation's careful review revealed that malaria, a seldom-mentioned scourge, also deserved its attention. The realization that a one-time expenditure of a few dollars on mosquito netting could save a child's life led to what is now a $1 billion effort that has helped millions of people.

Nonprofits, large and small, have embraced the return on investment approach. Teen pregnancy prevention agencies measure the cost per reduced teen birth of various prevention efforts; over time, they drop the less effective programs, but they drop the more expensive ones as well. Despite its acceptance in the social service world, however, public schools often seem uncomfortable with the concept of ROI.

Management of Pushback

In some districts, the idea of measuring return on investment in education can be uncomfortable. When I was superintendent, I was asked to approve a $150,000 purchase of new materials for our elementary writing program. Before answering, I asked how many students would be using the new materials and what gains we might expect in writing ability. The angry response surprised me: "It's just an update to our existing materials, so I don't expect anything will change. Moreover, the question is offensive. If only one student benefits, then that should be enough."

Because we were anticipating a zero academic return on investment, I refused to approve the purchase. I decided to use this example as a teaching moment, and actually sketched out the formula and shared the concept with my colleague. Huge mistake. The idea and the discussion were so upsetting that voices were raised and ugly words uttered. Undeterred, a few weeks later I shared the example, the concept, and the malaria story with my entire leadership team. Bigger mistake. I was greeted by dead silence, questioning stares, and much squirming. One person finally said what was on most people's minds: "I hope we never do anything so businesslike, so antichild, and so unethical in this district!" I was stunned. I was trying to do the most good, given limited funds. How was this unethical?

The discussion had poisoned my working relationship with my leadership team, so I reached out to an organizational consultant with extensive experience in K–12 education, nonprofits, and the private sector. I started to share the story, and within two sentences, he was able to predict what happened. Since he knew many on my team, I assumed that he had already heard the story, but he hadn't. He knew because it was predictable.

The consultant has been coaching superintendents, principals, central office staff, and leadership teams for thirty years. He was a big fan of personality profiles like the well-known Myers-Briggs. He also uses a test that gauges a person's values. It assesses what motivates people and reveals their underlying value system. It also maps the results to national norms. One of the values measured is *utility*, which is essentially a surrogate term for return on investment. People who score high on utility prioritize "a good value." They implicitly consider results and cost simultaneously, unable to appreciate, say, a good meal that was overpriced. It was no surprise that I—as a former business executive with an MBA, training in engineering, and an appreciation for cost-effective solutions—valued utility. What *was* surprising was that nearly none of the seventeen members of my leadership team did.

In fact, they didn't just not care about utility, they actually disliked it. I was counseled to stop talking about helping kids and saving money in the same meeting. I swallowed my pride, kept the calculations to myself, and regained the trust and support of my team.

A Challenge for Solomon

Beyond personal belief systems, there is also a practical reason why many districts shy away from A-ROI: it creates lists of winners and losers. In fact, its very purpose is to help rank various uses of funds to help districts decide which efforts are worth expanding and which should shrink. This is very uncomfortable in a K–12 culture that values getting along. Like King Solomon splitting the baby, everybody getting something seems to please everyone. Ironically, the point of that parable is that half a baby should please no one. In hundreds of budget discussions, I have seen eager consensus form for across-the-board spending cuts because these are the "fairest" reductions. I remember the anguish of my team when academic return on investment analysis revealed that our English intervention program was expensive and relatively ineffective, while our similar math efforts were more successful and lower in cost. Rather than celebrating that we had identified what works and what doesn't, nearly everyone felt terrible for the English department. As one person said, "I wish we didn't know the results; now we have no choice but to cut back on the English efforts. I'm so sorry." A-ROI won't win many friends, but how much impact can it have on the budget? A lot!

Identify Underfunded Areas

One of the most powerful benefits of the A-ROI concept is that it will highlight areas that are currently underfunded. During tight financial times, there is a tendency to try to hold on to as much as possible of what is already in place, and expanding programs takes a back seat. If districts want to raise achievement, then they likely need more of something. A high A-ROI can help sell the expanded effort. If they apply A-ROI to elementary reading, many districts will find that they are underspending in this critical area.

Reading Matters

I have never met an elementary school principal, director of curriculum, or superintendent who hasn't understood the importance of students reading on grade level by third grade. Based on this belief, my district shifted resources from less critical areas to support a combined special education and general education elementary reading program based on the National Reading Panel's recommendations. The impact was huge. Prior to the reform effort, the district estimated that only 10 percent of struggling elementary readers who started the school year below grade level reached grade level by year's end. After the reform efforts, over 65 percent of struggling readers became proficient readers during the school year. Overall, in grades K–5, the number of struggling readers declined by 68 percent, with 92.5 percent of students reading at grade level.

Most other districts, however, bemoan the fact that they don't have the time or financial resources to provide intensive support to struggling readers. The A-ROI model becomes a tool to help shift funds toward reading, especially when costs and benefits are rolled up over time, not just for a single year.

Consider an investment in reading support. In an elementary school of four hundred students, an intensive reading support program that provides coaching to classroom teachers and thirty minutes a day of extra help from a certified reading teacher to struggling students would cost about $250,000. Assuming one hundred students are struggling, this is $2,500 per student each year. In my experience, high-quality instruction and remediation can help students reach grade level in two to three years, which comes to $7,500 over the life of the intervention.

Failure to have a strong, early-intervention reading program leads to special education referrals, and in turn, special education services. In real estate, as the adage goes, only three things matter: location, location, location. Likewise, to raise the achievement of students with special needs, only three things matter: reading, reading, reading.

- Nationwide, reading is the core challenge for 40 percent of all students in special education.[2]
- Fully 80 percent of students nationwide with the designation *SLD* (specific learning disability) struggle with reading. SLD is the largest disability group, accounting for over 40 percent of students receiving special education services.[3]
- A student who can't read on grade level by third grade is four times less likely to graduate by age nineteen than a child who does read proficiently by that time. Add poverty to the mix, and a student is thirteen times less likely to graduate on time than his or her proficient, wealthier peer, but 89 percent of

students in poverty who did read on level by third grade graduated on time.[4]

- Reading is the gateway to all other learning. Social studies, English, and science cannot be mastered without strong reading skills. Even today's math instruction is word-problem-intensive.
- Schools with effective general education reading programs see referrals to special education drop by half.

The cost to serve a student with mild to moderate special needs averages about $5,000 a student each year based on my organization's studies (much higher if co-teaching is embraced, but more on that later). Since students almost never exit special education, the services may last ten years, for a lifetime cost of $50,000.

Beyond the dollars, worse yet, few special education students make even a year's progress each year, so the gap between general education and special education students grows as they enter middle and high school. Still worse, in a typical district, only about 10 percent of elementary students with special needs receive extra help in reading through special education, and, in this example, 25 percent of students will get extra help through general education. That's two and half times more students helped!

At this point, the A-ROI model can be applied conceptually or literally. Table 5.1 shows the big picture.

As you can see, even without a calculator, a dollar spent on early reading intervention helps more than twice as many students reach grade

Table 5.1

Conceptual view of reading academic return on investment

	General education reading intervention	Special education reading intervention
Learning	A lot	Much less
Number of students helped	100	40
Dollars spent over time	$750,000	$2,000,000

level and eventually graduate and go to college, while spending much less. A more detailed view might look like table 5.2.

Any way you look at it, investment in effective general education reading intervention makes a lot of sense, but where do you find the money for reading coaches and reading teachers? The answer is to shift dollars from all other efforts that have a lower A-ROI.

Behavior Management

Behavior management is another area where districts chronically underinvest, in part because they aren't considering return on investment. A-ROI can show that paying more for highly skilled staff is actually less expensive than paying less for lower-skilled paraprofessionals and could transform the lives of many students with behavior disabilities. Let's set the scene. About 80 percent of principals have reported on surveys conducted by my organization that the number of students with significant behavior needs has increased over the last five years. This isn't just unruly "boys being boys," but students with autism or with significant emotional and mental health disabilities acting out, leading to serious classroom disruptions.

Most districts address this growing challenge with an ever-expanding army of paraprofessionals. These relatively low-cost helpers monitor

Table 5.2

Numeric view of reading academic return on investment

	General education reading intervention	Special education reading intervention
Increase in student learning	1.5 years growth/year	0.8 years growth/year
Number of students helped	100	40
Dollars spent per year	$2,500	$5,000
Number of years of spending	3	10
Total dollars spent per student	$7,500	$50,000
Total dollars spent over time	$750,000	$2,000,000
Academic return on investment (per $10,000 spent)	4.5	0.02

students' behavior and remove them to the hallway when tempers flare. On one level, problem solved. The classroom instruction continues, and a low-cost employee helps the student. The multiyear A-ROI framework should force districts to ask, "Is it really a low-cost solution, and is it really helping students?"

First, the cost: the number of paraprofessionals in schools had risen to over seven hundred thousand in 2006 (the latest available data). This means paraprofessionals account for almost a quarter (22 percent) of all instructional staff in US schools.[5] Many of these positions were added to address behavior needs. In some districts, one-third to one-half of all aides are designated for behavior. In a midsized district of five thousand students, this could equal $1.5 million a year. A large urban district might spend $10 million on aides for behavior support. While each individual position is low cost, at least compared to a teacher, in total the dollars are big. Schools have so many aides because once an aide is assigned to a student with behavior issues, the help is likely to be needed for years.

Paraprofessionals seem like a reasonable response to students with behavior needs. Rightfully, districts want to include these students in the general education setting, but at the same time don't want outbursts to disrupt the learning of other students. Aides, unfortunately, are just a Band-Aid for the student. Rather than learning how to prevent outbursts or cope with frustration, these students learn that when they don't want to be in class, they should act out. Bad behavior creates a positive result. After graduation, this learned response creates great difficulty in college or at work, because while the aide may hug the student on graduation day, she doesn't stay with him for the rest of his life. The typical model of support will get a student through the day, but not necessarily through life. Since this response is not great for kids or the budget, it has a low return on investment.

What's a better solution? Hiring a skilled behaviorist, who earns much more than an aide, actually has a much better ROI. Behaviorists study in detail what triggers a student's outbursts, identify early warning signs, and create a behavior plan. This may include changing the environment (sitting away from a noisy heater, for example, which can be very upsetting to students with Asperger's), coaching the teacher in avoiding triggering events (such as unintentionally embarrassing a student who doesn't know the answer to a question), and teaching the student how to self-regulate. A few days or weeks of this high-level intervention can replace years of paraprofessional support and better prepare these student for productive lives despite their disabilities.

I have seen behaviorists work miracles. Students who seemed too violent to stay in school learned to avoid and regulate their outbursts. The What Works Clearinghouse, an initiative of the US Department of Education's Institute of Education Sciences (IES) and a trusted source of scientific evidence for what works in education, includes behavior management strategies as one of only fourteen topics with broad enough evidence of effectiveness to warrant a full-length guide. But despite behaviorists' great success rate and much need, most districts don't employ them. Why? The most common reason is that districts can't afford such costly help in tough times. A multiyear A-ROI review, however, would show they can't afford to *not* hire them!

Identify Costly or Less-Effective Uses of Scarce Funds

If academic return on investment is suggesting more money for reading teachers, reading coaches, and behaviorists, then it only seems fair to also use the tool to identify less-effective or less-cost-effective efforts, which can be reduced to free up the needed funds. Special education academic support is an area full of such possibilities. The large and lingering achievement gap between students with mild learning disabilities and their nondisabled peers suggests that the current common strategies for supporting students with mild learning disabilities aren't working well:

- Young people with disabilities drop out of high school at twice the rate of their peers.[6]
- Enrollment rates of students with disabilities in higher education are 50 percent lower than enrollment among the general population.[7]

Moving toward more effective and cost-effective models of helping students with special education needs is a true win-win—more learning and less spending. Helping students with mild to moderate disabilities is characterized by wild variation in approaches, much spending, and only limited learning. Few would question why districts, parents, and students should want better outcomes, despite ever-increasing expenditures. My consulting work in more than fifty districts, plus data from primary research covering nearly two thousand additional school systems, indicates that tradition, personal preference, and gut feeling often drive the choice of a "service delivery model" (aka strategy) for academic support. Our studies have found that schools tend to adopt and cling to one of a half-dozen strategies for helping students with learning disabilities. When staff members are asked why they do x, the answer is typically, "Because we always have," or "We did it in the district I came from." When they're asked if x is better than y or z, the answer is always, "I definitely think so, but I can't prove it."

The choice of strategy can have a big impact on kids and the budget. In my district, by changing the service delivery model, we closed the special education–general education achievement gap at the high school by 65 percent and nearly tripled the number of students with special needs scoring proficient or better in math and English, while spending less. Other districts we've studied could save $15 million to $25 million a year, depending on their choice of service delivery model. With the stakes so high, in terms of both student learning and expense, detailed A-ROI analysis makes sense.

Use A-ROI to Improve Special Education Outcomes

Most schools use one of the three most popular service delivery models to provide academic support to students with special needs:

- *Push-in.* A special education teacher joins a general education class to support a few children with special needs (co-teaching is a form of push-in support).
- *Pull-out.* Students with special needs are pulled together to receive extra help outside the general education classroom (resource room is a form of pull-out).
- *Double general education classes.* Struggling students attend two classes a day in a particular course, both taught by a general education teacher.

So which strategy has the highest academic return on investment? All school districts are different, but the experience of districts my organization has studied can help answer the question. The research indicates that push-in has the lowest return—more expense, less learning, and fewer students helped. Because each classroom in the sample districts typically has just two or three students with an IEP per general education classroom, when a special education teacher goes into the room for an hour, he can help just two or three students at a time. If this teacher works in five classes a day, he helps about fifteen students a year. Assuming that the average teacher compensation package (including benefits) is $75,000, that's $5,000 per student helped.

The pull-out model makes it easier to group students. With a typical group size of five students, a pull-out teacher running five classes a day can serve a total of twenty-five students a year, bringing the cost down to $3,000 per student.

Now for the final common option, double general education classes. Even a small general education class has fifteen students, so adding an extra teacher to teach five classes supports a total of seventy-five students, and brings the cost to just $1,000 per student helped. In the double class model, the student gives up an elective or a study hall to get an extra period of math or English. When a student needs support in both subjects, she may get half a year extra of each. Many elementary schools provide a second dose of reading each day for struggling students, which is a variation on this theme.

Focus on Results for Students with Special Needs

I suspect that some readers are ready to put the book down at this point. It can seem heartless to reduce learning to dollars spent per student. If we stop here, this isn't good education—it isn't education at all! It does raise the question, however: do the more expensive options create more learning? Research suggests just the opposite.

My organization's work includes extensive classroom visits, and often the researchers observe that during push-in, the costliest option, it is hard for students with special needs to make gains. The second teacher (a special education teacher) often isn't strong in the content. So if a special education student struggling in math has a question, he asks a nonmath teacher, whereas the general education students ask the certified math teacher. If the special education teacher responds with a long explanation or mini-lesson, the student will miss the core instruction; no one can listen to two teachers at once. Lastly, in nearly all the districts studied, the push-in model provides struggling students with just one period of math each day, just like their nonstruggling peers. These struggling students need extra time to remediate previous years' deficits while mastering this year's content. High spending and limited learning yields a low academic return on investment.

The pull-out model addresses some of these shortcomings. The student gets a full math class, and then extra help in a resource room each day. Still, the instructor isn't a math teacher. In most of the schools studied, this extra help is noncategorical; students who struggle in math, language arts, and other subjects are grouped together, often across multiple grades. This hodgepodge makes formal instruction impossible. The class often becomes homework help in a study-hall mode.

The final option provides two periods of general education instruction from a content-strong teacher. This guarantees quality instruction and ensures that the supplemental time is closely connected to the core lessons. In my district, we shifted from push-in and pull-out to double general education classes. The academic achievement of students with special needs increased dramatically in a few years. For example, the number of students with IEPs who reached tenth-grade proficiency in math and English nearly tripled. Three times the learning at one-fifth the cost—that's a win for kids and taxpayers.

The analysis is clear. In our sample of districts, push-in (including co-teaching) was more expensive and less effective than the alternatives; it had a lower academic return on investment. It is somewhat understandable that some districts choose this option, despite the low academic return on investment. There are many intellectually appealing aspects to co-teaching, and it is often called "the best of both worlds." What is less understandable is how many districts stick with this strategy even though their own data shows it to be both expensive and ineffective.

One district studied had a top-notch data analyst and a perfectly controlled test. Half of its schools did co-teaching, and half did the much less expensive pull-out resource room model. Based on years of individual student growth data, the district learned that students in the very expensive co-taught classrooms made no more, and perhaps slightly fewer, gains than students receiving less-expensive alternatives. I thought this would be welcomed news given that the district faced major funding shortfalls, was laying off staff, and claimed it couldn't afford all the reading teachers it needed. Despite the data, though, not much changed. Schools that had co-taught still did, while no new school would ever take up the practice, given the results.

Embrace Experimentation

It seems that to stop co-teaching would require the aforementioned district to acknowledge that it made a mistake, but to continue with an ineffective, costly practice soothed the feelings of teachers and administrators alike. This example raises the most important point of applying A-ROI—districts need a cultural shift that embraces experimentation and at the same time gleefully abandons what doesn't work in a blame-free way. I often shared with my staff, "There is no shame in doing something that doesn't work; the shame is in not knowing it doesn't work." I never expected all of our new programs to be effective. That's right; I regularly tried ideas that I had doubts about, while others may have championed them. The key was that after six months or a year, we would all have the data to know what was and wasn't working.

The case of dueling remediation strategies in my district is a good case in point. The high school English department had become enamored with a "high-touch" combination advisory and tutoring model for writing intervention. Students would meet in very small groups of one or two with an English teacher for three hours a week. They would spend equal time creating a relationship as well as getting help on their writing assignments. I liked the idea. The data said that a connection between student and teacher was critical, and we hand-picked top instructors for the program. It was an expensive model, given the low teacher-to-student ratio, but I and others thought it worthwhile, despite an average cost of $3,500 per student helped.

Out of a sense of equity, I offered to fund a similar program for math. The math director didn't like the idea. She felt we needed to reach many more students and that reteaching skill deficits mattered more than homework help. The math extra help program created an extra class of twenty students that met five times a week for half a year. It included small-group instruction, new software that pinpointed trouble areas, and computer-generated practice lessons. This struck me as disconnected "drill and kill." I would never have funded it, but it was much less expensive than the English program at $1,000 per student helped, and the culture of equity forced me to do something for math. The one condition I imposed on both programs was that we would track the results in detail, including establishing baseline data on grades, common formative assessment results, attendance, and state test scores. Pre- and post-testing was mandatory.

The data was striking. Students in the math program made one and a half to two years' progress, attendance was great, and the class was so well received that a few kids even snuck into it. "I finally get it" was an often-uttered comment. Our (my) beloved English program had spotty attendance and no improvement in grades on the writing assignments. Given the great cost, we scaled back and tweaked the program, hoping to find the missing components. Year two was no better than year one, while the math effort continued to work miracles. The answer was obvious: we needed to model English remediation after the math program. We did, and costs dropped and learning increased.

The most important aspect of this story isn't that the English program wasn't effective—not every idea will work. The shocking part is how good the English program looked during walk-throughs and interviews with the staff. It seemed and felt like a success, but it wasn't. Without baseline and ongoing data collection, it is very likely that the English program would have persisted, and as budgets shrank, the math effort, due to only halfhearted support from the superintendent, would have been cut.

Spread Success to Many Students

Academic return on investment can also let a district determine if a good idea is just too expensive to actually be a good idea. For example, take the Reading Recovery program, the very successful reading intervention program that targets struggling first-graders. The data is impressive—Reading Recovery helps students through intensive support provided by skilled and well-trained teachers. Many districts have made large commitments to this program because it is effective. These same districts, however, haven't asked themselves whether it is also *cost-effective.*

Reading Recovery is provided only to a single student at a time. It is not uncommon that a full-time Reading Recovery teacher will serve only ten to twelve students a year. In many districts I have studied, this program, with its low student-to-teacher ratio (a class size of one), consumes the entire reading intervention budget. That means no extra help in kindergarten, second grade, third grade, and above. This lack of extra help leads to more referrals to special education and its associated expenses.

If the funds devoted to Reading Recovery were devoted to reading teachers providing support based on the National Reading Panel, each teacher could help thirty to forty students instead of ten to twelve, allowing extra reading help in all grades K–5. So which is better? Each district should apply the A-ROI methodology to find out for itself. Both strategies make sense, but which one is more effective and more cost-effective?

Make More Informed Trading-Down Decisions

Beyond helping choose between different programs, the A-ROI framework is helpful when considering the options for trading down, discussed in chapter 2. Take, for example, speech and language assistants—the lesser-trained, lower-cost cousins to speech and language therapists. Most discussions on whether to use fully licensed therapists or assistants focus on arguments like "Therapists are better trained, so they are better for kids." According to the American Speech-Language-Hearing Association (ASHA), the therapists' professional association, assistants are equally effective as therapists in delivering instruction, so long as the therapists diagnose the need and monitor student progress.

There are many other ways and places to apply the concept of A-ROI. Class size decisions are one such example, as discussed in chapter 4. Other important areas that would benefit from such a review include:

- Specific professional development efforts
- Common planning time

- Professional learning communities
- Dropout prevention efforts
- Small schools
- Coaching
- Remediation and intervention efforts

Measure Success

One superintendent I know was fond of saying, "The hardest part of the job is you don't know what worked for seventy-five years. We have to wait and see how the lives of our students turn out." This is a polite way of saying, "We can't measure the effectiveness of our efforts, so gut feeling (aka professional judgment) must do." It is not fair to students to continue with efforts that are ineffective, and taxpayers also want each dollar to make a difference. It is incumbent on districts to *not* wait seventy-five years to know what's working and what's not. This requires robust systems to measure achievement in real time.

There are four ways to measure effectiveness, which is the numerator in the A-ROI formula. Finding the dollars spent, the denominator, is usually straightforward accounting—but remember to use fully loaded costs.

Run Controlled Tests

The best way to know what works is to incorporate program evaluation into the rollout. When starting a new program, purposefully plan to test effectiveness by creating controlled experiments that isolate all the variables except one. In one district, as mentioned earlier in this chapter, such an experiment happened by accident when one-half of the elementary schools used co-teaching and one-half could only afford to provide resource room support to students with special needs. An analysis of student growth in math and English over multiple years revealed that students in co-taught classrooms gained at the same rate as their peers who didn't receive this costly intervention. This data suggested redeploying the many millions invested in co-teaching into other efforts. A controlled test needn't be accidental, however.

Just as drug companies are required to test the effectiveness of all new medicines, districts should test the effectiveness of new (and existing) programs and pedagogies. Drug testing is a good model. Pharmaceutical companies aren't allowed to give everyone in a trial a pill to see if they get better. Half the sample gets nothing but a placebo. When rolling out a new program, half the teachers can use the new material or approach for a year or two, and results can be compared to the control group. I know this seems complicated and perhaps unfair, but it seems even more unfair to not know if an approach is working or if it's better than some alternative.

Search for Pockets of Evidence

Districts have more controlled tests going on right now than they realize. For example, as superintendent, I asked a data analyst to identify classrooms, grades, or schools that significantly outperformed the rest of the district, taking demographic factors into account. The findings were striking. Our highest-poverty school had made steady gains in reading, while other schools stayed flat. Donning our Sherlock Holmes caps, we asked why. After much interviewing and observing, it turned out that the reading gains came from a relentless focus on phonics, expanded time for instruction, and replacing noncertified tutors with fewer, but more skilled, teachers.

In many districts, each classroom teacher is trying something different. Each school may have a unique approach, program, schedule, or staffing model. With a bit of data analysis, districts can spot highly effective efforts by looking at results from individual teachers or schools.

The trick in doing this well is controlling for a few key variables. If school A outperforms school B, is it because there is less poverty in school A? Could it be that school B has much more transient students or houses a substantial number of special-needs programs? A handful of districts use sophisticated regression analysis to sort all this out. If you don't have a PhD number cruncher on staff, there are a few simple methods for discerning what is truly effective versus just easier to educate students.

When comparing results, remove the following from the sample:

- Students who have been in the school less than a year
- Students who have severe special needs

- Students with very limited English proficiency—say, those in the country for two years or less

Then compare:

- Students from poverty in one school to impoverished students in another school
- Students not from impoverished backgrounds to like students
- Students with limited English proficiency to each other

Within these comparison groups, as figure 5.1 illustrates, better results are more likely due to adult actions than a child's life story. By breaking the schools into three groups based on student poverty, we can compare schools with similar types of students. Within the highest-poverty group, one school stands out as significantly outperforming peer schools. In the middle group, one school also stands out. It is worth noting that none of the schools in group 1 may be best-practice schools, even though they have the highest proficiency rates. The star in group 2 performed as well as all the schools in the low-poverty group, despite its more challenging students.

The data alone won't prove that one approach is more effective than another, but it focuses the investigation. Often, the differences are glar-

Figure 5.1

Searching for best-practice schools

Comparing proficiency and poverty rates

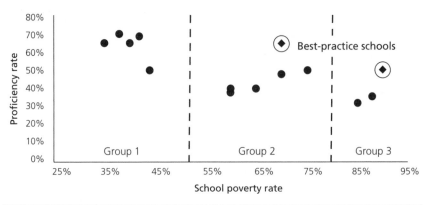

ing. When one district applied this analysis to elementary math scores on a teacher-by-teacher basis, it identified a number of seemingly high-performing teachers. The district then interviewed and observed all of these teachers in an effort to discover what made them great. It didn't take Scotland Yard to find out why their results were so strong. Even though the identified high performers worked in different schools and for the most part didn't know one another, they had a number of practices in common—practices that didn't exist in most other classrooms. For example, all of the high-performing teachers:

- Had a lifelong love of math
- Had a deep conceptual understanding of math
- Taught math (formally) for sixty minutes a day, without exception
- Taught at least three ways to the right answer, a strategy that recognizes that different students approach math problems differently
- Wove extra math into all other activities, such as having students count off by threes when they lined up to go to recess

This contrasted greatly to the district's typical elementary teacher, who loved reading more than math, taught only thirty or forty-five minutes of math a day (skipping it altogether in case of an assembly), and was completely unfamiliar with the "three ways to a right answer" strategy. This research convinced the district not to buy a new math curriculum—since these high-fliers got great results using the same textbooks as everyone else—but rather to shift the focus to increasing content knowledge, expanding the "multiple roads to a right answer" approach, and changing who it hired in the future.

Open the Treasure Chest of Data in Common Formative Assessments

Because of the standards movement and response to intervention, schools today administer many common formative assessments and do lots of progress monitoring. A *common formative assessment* is any test that is given to the entire grade or subject. This can be home-grown assessments like Friday spelling words, or common final exams. It can also be purchased exams, like unit tests in the textbook, or nationally normed products like DIBELS (dynamic indicators of basic early literacy skills). The primary purpose of these exams is to help teachers improve and personalize instruction, but one by-product is mounds of data that can help measure program effectiveness. If districts engage in *pretesting*, the practice of giving final tests at the start as well as at the end of a unit or course, then growth in student achievement can be measured and compared as well.

Conducting this type of analysis may seem overwhelming, and might seem like it requires a lot of manpower and technology, but I have been surprised by how often it's done without the superintendent even knowing or asking. More than a few directors of assessment and accountability have shared with me something like the following: "You know, we have all of this common formative assessment data in the computer, like DIBELS, developmental reading assessment (DRA), and pre- and post-unit math tests. I had the computer compare end-of-year scores to end-of-prior-year scores (or pretests to post-tests), calculate the gains, and then sort by teacher or building. I made sure to control for demographics. I identified where big gains were happening, and the next time I was in the school, I asked around to see what was special. Often, it was obvious."

Know That Zero Is an Answer

The goal is to find out what works best, but knowing that something isn't working at all puts that question to rest. As obvious as this may seem, districts don't always check to see whether an effort has failed. When I was superintendent, we created many measures of success. Some were easy—for instance, our dropout prevention program was designed to help students graduate, and our English remediation class was designed to raise writing achievement. Armed with these clear definitions of success, we were able to measure whether the programs were working. We discovered that over three years, 96 percent of students in the dropout prevention program dropped out of school.

We also learned that students' grades on essays did not improve after one year of intensive writing support. We learned that these programs had zero A-ROI and needed to be revamped. If they had demonstrated some success, it would have been harder to compare them to alternatives, but zero is an actionable answer.

Few districts knowingly continue with an effort that has zero impact, but many such programs are still funded year after year. There are a few reasons for this, but the two most common are having no clear measure of success and making no formal effort to track the results. When I asked how we should measure the success of our dropout prevention efforts, the first answer was, "If the kids feel welcomed in my classroom, then we are a success." Others added, "I can see success in their eyes. They have a certain engagement and energy." Happiness, not graduation, seemed to be the unofficial measure of success. I insisted that a high school diploma or GED spelled triumph, but no one associated with the program had tracked this data. It only took the guidance department thirty minutes to pull the records and shine the light on an ineffective program.

Use Growth Data

In most cases, it is best to measure student growth rather than absolute achievement when assessing effectiveness. Growth data, or value-added data, measures improvement rather than mastery. While mastery is the goal, A-ROI wants to find the efforts that are improving student outcomes. Fortunately, many states are starting to calculate this information on NCLB tests, and fairly simple pre- and post-testing or just periodic testing can allow districts to calculate their own internal growth scores.

Let's assume two teachers are using different strategies to teach reading. If Mrs. Smith's student, on average, outscored Mrs. Jones's on a nationally normed reading comprehension test, this doesn't mean Mrs. Smith's efforts were more effective. What if Mrs. Jones's students, on average, entered her class six months behind in reading, unlike Mrs. Smith's students? It is much less ambiguous if we know that most students in Mrs. Smith's class made fourteen months of progress, while Mrs. Jones's class only made eight months of growth.

A CRAZY IDEA?

Don't Let the School Nurse Dispense
Unproven Medicine to Sick Children

This seems absolutely crazy; obviously, we would never let the school nurse hand out medicine that hasn't been tested by the FDA. We wouldn't allow this even faced with pushback arguing that relying on a doctor's prescription was insulting to the professionalism of our dedicated school nurses. It's equally unlikely that, in an effort to lower health care costs, we would advocate letting the pharmaceutical companies stop all that expensive double-blind testing and let doctors prescribe whatever they think is effective. Yes, these are truly crazy ideas, but many schools do something similar when it comes to reading, writing, and math.

Many districts leave the decision of what and how to teach up to each teacher. Some districts leave what to teach up to each school. Despite this professional freedom, few schools measure what's working and what's not. In more than 90 percent of the schools and districts I visit, there is more variation between classroom instruction and content than there is measurement of student success.

I remember sitting around a table with six elementary principals in one district and asked them all to describe their reading programs. In turn, they each described completely different materials, schedules, approaches, assessments, and even staffing patterns (some used noncertified tutors, some volunteers, and others certified reading teachers). They chuckled at how different they all were, and commented that they appreciated the trust placed in them by the district, which didn't impose a one-size-fits-all model. I then asked which school had the best growth in reading achievement. After an uncomfortable silence, they said they didn't know (despite having mountains of common formative assessment data). They felt a bit embarrassed, but I assured them that I already knew that they wouldn't be able to answer the question. "How could you know?" one asked. "It's simple," I said, "If you knew which school was most effective at teaching reading, then even without central office pressure, you would have all copied what worked best, and there wouldn't be so much variation between buildings!"

So the actual crazy idea is not to give untested medicine to kids, but to measure and share what's working so that effective ideas get copied. Some schools have embraced data walls, where student growth by teacher is posted on the walls of the faculty lunchroom. I was having lunch in one such room and noticed that Mrs. T. had outstanding results compared to her colleagues, and Ms. D. had almost no growth from her students. I figured this out in less time than it took to sip my Diet Coke. I asked the teachers how it felt to have such data.

They said that at first it was unsettling, and the union had pushed to keep teacher names off the charts. When they saw the results, however, they all wanted to know who was so successful so they could copy and learn what worked. Mrs. D., especially, wanted to change her practices. She had thought her kids were learning, but now she knew they weren't.

Focus on measuring student growth and cost-effectiveness will—just by sharing that data—drive teachers, principals, and school boards to move to best practices. Like Mrs. D., no teacher is knowingly ineffective, but unknowingly some are.

6

Rethinking Special Education

ACHIEVING BETTER OUTCOMES
AT LOWER COSTS

No district can create smarter budgets without tackling the
twin challenges of raising achievement for students with special
needs while reducing costs. Fortunately, dozens of best-practice
strategies exist for rethinking the roles and schedules of para-
professionals, therapists, special education teachers, and
elementary reading staff.

"That's illegal," she said, and *That's immoral,* she thought. Not exactly the reaction I was hoping for after my speech on raising achievement while lowering costs for students with special needs. It would have been easy to dismiss the comment if it came from a nervous parent, but these were the sentiments of a sharp, financially savvy superintendent with big budget shortfalls and ballooning special education costs.

Managing the special education budget is both the same and different from managing all other types of costs in a school district. Most of the strategies are agnostic—they work with special education and general education alike—and special education examples have been provided throughout this book.

There are a few strategies that are particular to special education and worth a deep dive. Despite escalating special education costs, districts tend to shy away from tackling the challenge of managing them. The good news is, districts can lower costs while helping students with disabilities.

There are a few topics that are still hard to discuss candidly in public; race may be the most uncomfortable topic to broach, but special education costs are a close second. In private, some parents and educators worry that the relentless increases in special education spending are pulling funds from general education. Parents of students with special needs worry that their children aren't at grade level, won't make it through college, or won't be able to keep a job. It seems no one is happy, but no one is talking, either. This lose-lose situation is just getting worse. The share of total US school budgets spent on special education has increased from 4 percent to 21 percent from 1970 to 2005.[1] The number of students with severe special needs continues to grow, even as the total number of students with disabilities moderates. From 2000 to 2009, the total number of children with special needs grew by less than 3 percent, but during the same period, students with more challenging disabilities like autism (up over 300 percent), developmental delay (up 73 percent) and other health impairments (up 128 percent)—which are often a surrogate for complex behavior issues—became a greater share of the children served in special education.[2] As budgets shrink, special education spending, which is protected by laws and lawyers, is seldom cut, leaving general education to feel all the pain.

The few bold school board members or superintendents who do try to tackle the subject are quickly attacked from all sides. Parents of children with special needs rightfully are concerned that "less" could be worse. Special education teachers view the discussion as balancing the budget on the backs of the neediest children. And many special education directors, concerned about compliance, stamp most cost-saving ideas as illegal ("OK, if you want to go to jail, we can look into it!"), and so the discussion ends.

Adopt a "Yes, We Can" Attitude for Doing More with Less

There was a time, not too long ago, when a mostly unknown, relatively inexperienced African American politician announced he wanted to be the next president of the United States. This seemed a far-fetched idea. About as outlandish as reining in special education costs while improving—greatly improving—student learning. The goal of this chapter is to show that spending more on special education hasn't helped struggling children, and that spending less money more wisely will help them.

That unlikely presidential candidate, Barack Obama, believed that the seemingly impossible was possible. After the first primary, he said:

> We know the battle ahead will be long, but always remember that no matter what obstacles stand in our way, nothing can stand in the way of the power of millions of voices calling for change. We have been told we cannot do this by a chorus of cynics. They will only grow louder and more dissonant in the weeks and months to come. We've been asked to pause for a reality check; we've been warned against offering the people of this nation false hope. But in the unlikely story that is America, there has never been anything false about hope. For when we have faced down impossible odds; when we've been told we're not ready, or that we shouldn't try, or that we can't, generations of Americans have responded with a simple creed that sums up the spirit of a people. Yes, we can. Yes, we can. Yes, we can.[3]

Can districts spend less and get better outcomes for students with special needs? Yes, we can. It is time to break the psychological linkage between spending and results, to acknowledge that past increases haven't been accompanied by subsequent gains, and to stop equating resources with caring. I have seen firsthand that districts can raise achievement and lower costs for students with special needs.

Don't Exempt Special Education from Scrutiny

There are four basic strategies for doing more with less in special education. The first is to apply all the concepts of prudent management outlined in this book (and elsewhere) to special education. As obvious as this sounds, special education is often exempt from practices and procedures applied elsewhere in the district. For example, some CFOs simply accept the proposed special education budget as is, while they are much more likely to question other requests. Outside contracts for special education services aren't always subject to as much scrutiny as other vendors, and even class size figures are seldom reviewed for special education programs, though general education class size figures are typically under the microscope.

Abandon Practices That Aren't Working

The second strategy is to do what works and stop doing what doesn't. Students with special needs get counted, classified, and reported a lot, but their learning doesn't. Special education is awash in paperwork, state and federal reports, and endless checks for compliance with regulations. Pretty much the only thing not measured is which practices, strategies, or programs are actually leading to learning. Spending money on what isn't effective is bad for kids and the budget. See chapter 5 for more details on how academic return on investment can be applied to special education.

Manage Staffing Details

The third strategy is also borrowed from general education, and is really just a twist on staffing to need, as discussed in chapter 4. Thoughtful workload analysis and staffing based on student requirements offers a big opportunity to lower the cost of special education, without taking a minute of teaching away from children.

Staffing and scheduling based on student need represents the largest opportunity to free up funds. Once student needs are documented in fine detail, thoughtful schedules can be built. This may not seem like a big idea, but better scheduling can reduce staffing requirements by 30 percent and total special education costs by 10 percent in many districts, without changing a single word in a single IEP and without reducing a single minute of services to a single student with a disability. The only catch is that you need a great deal of detailed information to take advantage of this opportunity, information that isn't always readily available.

Let's assume five hundred students with special needs require speech and language services as part of their IEP (individual education program), which is the legally binding agreement between school and parent that outlines the special services to be provided to a student with a disability. So how many speech and language therapists are needed? Unlike the case in general education—where, if five hundred students need high school math, it's easy to calculate that with a class size of twenty-five, and five classes a day for each teacher, you'd need exactly four teachers— it's not so simple to figure out how many speech and language therapists are needed. Some of the five hundred students with special needs require thirty minutes a week of service, while others need ninety minutes. Some can be placed in groups of three or four, while others must be seen alone. Even for students who can be helped in a small group, there is no guarantee that another age-appropriate child in the same school needs the same help. In short, knowing that five hundred students need speech and language therapy doesn't tell you much, but it's all most directors or superintendents know when budgeting their staff.

If a computer (or a person) did tally up all of the student needs and mapped out the logical groupings, a district can convert the five hundred students into, say, 250 hours each week of therapist time. Few districts invest the effort to crunch numbers in this detail. Instead, some districts assign one therapist to each school and more if it's a big school. When therapists get overloaded, they complain loudly, and eventually the district hires more staff. More frugal districts assign one therapist to multiple schools, but it is still mostly a guess as to whether it should be two schools or three.

I have worked with a number of districts that took the time (or bought software) to analyze all the IEPs, crunch the numbers, build the groups, and staff accordingly. In most cases, they achieved savings of about 30 percent or more. The gain is so large because, without detailed planning, some schools are overstaffed and others are understaffed. Therapists with light workloads stay quiet, while overloaded staff clamor for hiring more therapists. Figure 6.1 shows just how inefficient therapist staffing is in a real district. Each bar represents the portion of the school week a therapist works with children. Some work as little as nine hours a week, while others are busy most of the time, serving children twenty-seven hours a week.

Figure 6.1

Portion of the week spent providing direct speech and language service to students

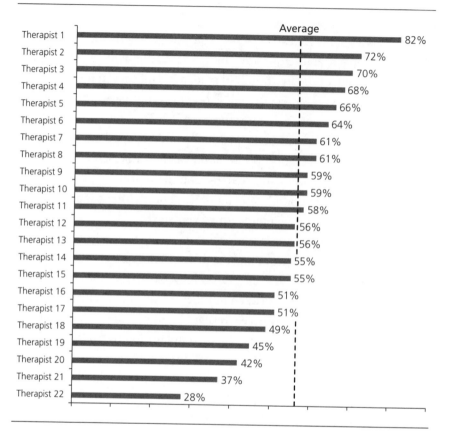

The savings in a midsized district of five thousand students can be $300,000 a year, while I have seen opportunities of many millions of dollars in larger districts. Keep in mind, not a single minute of service has been taken away from any child, and not a single IEP changed—just more detailed scheduling, thoughtful grouping, and efficient staffing allocation.

The situation with the staffing of special education teachers is similar, except on a grander scale. As figure 6.2 shows, in a midsized district the range of workloads for each special education teacher is also quite variable. Through better allocation planning, fewer teachers could serve

Figure 6.2

Portion of week special education teachers instruct students

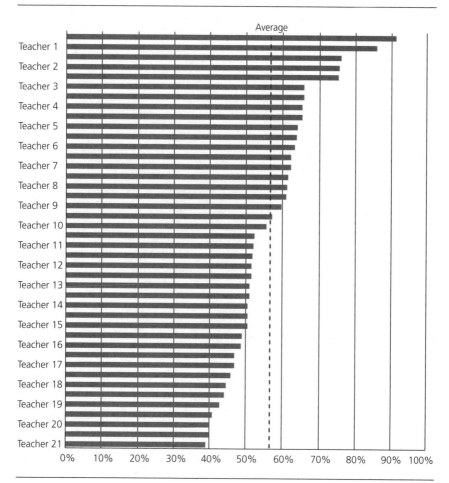

the students in the district. The savings in this midsized district would top $1 million a year.

Schedule Effectively

Good scheduling, the fourth strategy for doing more with less, can also reduce the number of special education paraprofessionals needed in a district. A paraprofessional is an assistant assigned to a student with special needs. In the past, it was very common to assign paraprofessionals one-on-one, which means an adult hovered near a single student all day, every day. Beyond the expense (typically $30,000–$40,000 a year, including benefits), this constant supervision isolated the child from his peers and encouraged the classroom teacher to pay less attention to the student, since she had her own "private teacher." The problem is, aides aren't teachers, and many aren't even college graduates. Over time, many districts have moved to shared aides, no longer mandating one-on-one support. Despite these changes, districts are often still overstaffed with too many paraprofessionals. In fact, there is now one paraprofessional for every four and a half teachers in the United States.[4] Why this overstaffing? Bad scheduling and bad information.

Scheduling matters. Let's say John and Jim both require a shared aide, are in second grade, and attend the Kennedy School. It seems like only one aide is required, but not if John and Jim are scheduled into different classrooms. Now two aides are needed! Many districts have no systems in place to ensure that students who should share an aide are in fact placed in the same classroom.

Effective scheduling is complex because student needs are complex. One student needs help in the morning for school phobia issues. Another needs help during math, a third needs help getting from one classroom to another, and a fourth struggles with social issues during unstructured times like lunch and recess. Collectively, all four need about twenty hours of help each week, which is about a half-time job. In many districts, four full-time staff members will be hired to take care of these students. Each might help other children as well, but few schools schedule part-time support. If you are thinking, *just don't hire four people*, think again. The math help conflicts with the early-morning assistance. Lunch and recess support overlap with helping a child move between classes.

Look at microscheduling. The lack of sophisticated scheduling leads to other wasteful practices. In most districts, paraprofessional support is assigned every day and usually all day long. Some children do need this round-the-clock support, but mostly it is driven by the ease of scheduling one adult to one room for a year. The most powerful example came from one midsized district. In some schools, children were assigned one-on-one paraprofessionals all day, every day. In the same district, other schools had virtually banned the one-on-one approach as not good for children, so all aides were shared, and as a result these schools had far fewer paraprofessionals. One school, however, had a master scheduler. A single teacher took it upon herself to maximize a student's chance for independence. Each year, she spent about three weeks in August creating detailed paraprofessional schedules. Rather than scheduling for the year, week, or day, she looked at her school's student need in thirty-minute increments. For example, Amy needed support in the mornings until 10 a.m., but not later. Jason needed help during reading, but not math. Sarah went to the learning lab for a few hours, and didn't need an aide then. Finally, the teacher coordinated with the principal to make sure the right children were assigned to each classroom.

The net result of this *microscheduling* was that the typical paraprofessional worked in six different rooms during the week, not just one, and the school needed two-thirds fewer aides. Keep in mind, not a single change was made to the students' IEPs. When the rest of the district adopted similar practices, it saved and avoided spending over $3 million, in the first two years, with lots more room for improvement.

I'm often asked, if the savings are so significant and there is no impact on students, why don't more schools embrace microscheduling? Good schedules require good information. They require a level of detail generally not available at the push of a button. Strangely enough, however, all the needed information *is* actually sitting in existing district databases.

Centralize and coordinate scheduling. Creating student-centered, cost-effective schedules also requires one person to schedule lots of people, virtually everyone in a given school. This conflicts with the prevailing ethos of classroom teachers, special education teachers, and therapists all as independent agents. Historically, everyone makes his or her own schedule, and taking away this authority can feel punitive or demeaning.

Unfortunately, thoughtful scheduling must be centralized and coordinated. For example, in most elementary schools I have visited, a schedule is created in this sequence:

1. Principal sets schedule for lunch and recess.
2. Principal sets schedule for art, music, PE, and library.
3. Teachers set their classroom schedules for major subjects like reading, math, etc.
4. Special education teacher tries to find times to work with students, but not during lunch, recess, core subjects, and maybe not during special subjects like art, music, PE, or library.
5. Speech therapist tries to find times that still remain.
6. Occupational therapist tries to find times still not taken.

Here's the rub. Steve and Sally should meet with the speech therapist together, but because they are in different classrooms, they aren't available at the same time. Each will be seen one-on-one, thus doubling the staffing requirements to serve these children.

Letting classroom teachers build schedules on their own often leads to huge inefficiencies as well. It is not uncommon for every teacher in the school to schedule reading from 9:00 a.m. to 10:30 a.m. and math from 11:00 a.m. to 12:00 p.m. Many teachers consider this peak learning time. Unfortunately, district guidelines prevent special education staff from pulling out a student during these core-subject time blocks. This in turn means that for half the day, all the special education staff members in a building do paperwork, testing, meetings, and other activities that don't require the student to be present!

Find a scheduling guru. Lastly, not all schools have someone who is skilled at creating a thoughtful, multidimensional, efficient schedule. The job usually falls to the principal or assistant principal, but there is no guarantee (or even likelihood) that this is their strong suit. I can empathize. I am the world's least able schedule maker. I have always relied on the kindness of others to help me schedule. I'm not alone. When I asked a large group of principals and special education teachers if they would like someone to help build their schedules, 80 percent said, "Yes, please! Scheduling is the bane of my existence." In a district of nine schools, for example, only two principals, one assistant principal, and one teacher were scheduling gurus. A few thousand dollars in stipends to have these master schedulers help their less skilled colleagues saved hundreds of thousands of dollars in staffing costs.

Building thoughtful schedules in special education requires the district leadership, not just special education leaders, to play a bigger role as well. The district leadership must set some guidelines. Should a typical special education teacher support twelve students on average, or twenty-four? Should a therapist spend fifteen hours per week on paperwork and meetings, or eight? While there are no right or wrong answers, the problem lies in the fact that there are seldom any formal answers at all.

I have asked scores of superintendents questions like "How many first-graders do you target in each classroom?" and "How many classes do math teachers have each day at the high school?" These are de facto staffing guidelines for general education. Every super knows the answer instantly. But to date, no superintendent and few directors of special education could answer the special ed equivalent.

Once thoughtful schedules are created for the entire district, it's easy to know how many special education staff members are needed in each building. By creating a centralized, thoughtful master schedule, a district can often meet all the student needs with 30 percent fewer staff. These findings apply to special education teachers, speech and language therapists, occupational therapists, and paraprofessionals—the majority of the special education budget.

Improve the Identification Process

For about half the districts in the country, there is a straightforward solution to reducing special education costs: stop overreferring students to special education. Don't worry, this is not taking away from kids in need. Read on.

It is odd that, forty-plus years after President Ford signed the first special education legislation, we still don't have a workable definition for the disabilities warranting special education services. This isn't just an academic or legal question, because every student incorrectly identified is likely to achieve less and cost more—a lose-lose proposition. Despite US Department of Education guidelines, thousands of precedents, and mountains of nationally normed tests, special education eligibility is mostly an "I know it when I see it" designation. For the staff involved, it may feel thoughtful and methodical, but the data says otherwise.

- In Pennsylvania, students are four times more likely to be diagnosed as learning disabled (SLD, the most common diagnosis) than in Kentucky.
- In districts with identical student demographics, one district may identify 24 percent of students as needing special education, another 15 percent, another 10 percent, and others 7 percent.
- Some districts stop most speech and language services by third grade, while others see the need continuing into high school.
- Nationally, about 13 percent of students are classified as qualifying for special education, while research by Tom Hehir suggests that about 6 percent of students have a true learning disability.[5] Tom should know: he is a professor at the Harvard Graduate School of Education, is the former director of special education for the Boston and Chicago public schools, and served as director of the US Department of Education's Office of Special Education Programs under Bill Clinton.

It can't be true that one district or state has four times as many learning-disabled kids as another similar district or state. Where a child goes to school dramatically impacts whether she "has" a disability, and thus whether she receives special education services.

Students overidentified for special education *are* struggling and in need of help—that's not in question—but they *are not* in need of special education. Overidentification isn't good; it isn't even benign. Too often I hear, "So what? We help a few more kids than we must." There are a few problems with this philosophy. The first is that special education services aren't overly effective in most districts given the persistent achievement gap between students with and without special needs.

Based on my work as a consultant looking at more than fifty school systems across the country, I have found that many districts confuse a struggling student with a disabled one. This is often because the district doesn't provide substantial services to help general education struggling students, so the only route for extra help is special education. Some principals call special education "the golden ticket," because it provides access to services not available otherwise.

If districts provided intensive, high-quality support in reading, writing, and math without requiring an IEP, kids and the budget would benefit. It turns out that special education is the most expensive way to help struggling students. Based on estimates from my research, serving an overidentified struggling student with mild to moderate needs will cost about $5,000 a year extra in special education for roughly ten years, for a total additional cost of $50,000. Effective general education intervention costs about $2,000 a year extra, and typically is only required for two to three years, costing no more than a total of $6,000 extra. Most importantly, the outcomes for the general education intervention are much better for the child, as well as less costly.

Good general education options plus clear criteria for eligibility will help students and the budget. To provide effective, intensive general education support, districts must find savings from existing special education spending to shift to these new, more effective, and more cost-effective efforts.

Serve More Children In-District

If some districts overidentify students with mild disabilities, they may also be underserving students with more severe special needs. Severe needs are often referred to as the ABCs of special education: autism, behavior, and cognitive impairment. The number of these high-needs students is growing.

In my experience, educators do not favor outsourcing or subcontracting, with one glaring exception. Many districts are happy to have others educate their neediest special education students. Students with autism, severe behavior needs, or low cognitive ability are often sent to special schools. Generically, these are called *out-of-district placements*, and they are the de facto form of outsourcing the education of some students with special needs. The prevalence of this practice varies greatly by state. Where it is a common practice, especially in the Northeast and Midwest, it serves neither students nor the budget well.

Size Doesn't Always Matter

The question of whether a district can effectively educate a high-needs student (such as one with nonverbal autism, behavior disorder, or significant cognitive impairment) is usually answered, "It depends on the size of the district"; that is, large districts can, and small districts cannot. The truth isn't that simple. Many sizable school districts, especially in the Northeast, send lots of students to expensive out-of-district schools. Conversely, districts with as few as two thousand students have high-quality programs to cost-effectively meet the needs of students with significant needs. Attitude and history play a bigger role than economies of scale. Although students with severe needs constitute a small portion of special education students, they account for about half of all special education spending in some districts. Most parents would prefer their child to be educated in a local school, be part of the community, and interact with nondisabled peers.

A study in Massachusetts showed that district size had no bearing on whether students with special needs were served inside or outside the district. For example, as figure 6.3 shows, many districts with just

Figure 6.3

Massachusetts students attending out-of-district placements (as a % of total district enrollment)

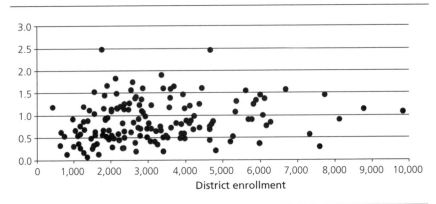

two thousand students served most students with severe needs in-house, while many districts with six thousand students had most of these students at out-of-district placements. All the districts in the oval have about the same percentage of students out of district. Every school system above the selected region has a substantial opportunity to serve more students in-district.

Even more compelling, some entire states have figured out how to serve students with severe special needs in-district. Schools in Connecticut, for example, send almost half as many students (adjusted for total enrollment) out-of-district than schools in Massachusetts, while Texan districts send out almost no students at all.

Cost and Quality Do Not Go Hand in Hand

Typically, a public school can provide an identical program, with the same staffing ratios and services, for about 40 percent less than an out-of-district placement. The savings come from lower costs for facilities, marketing, and transportation. In many cases, a program can break even with two children enrolled and create savings with three students, as detailed in table 6.1.

The savings are significant, but not at the cost of quality. The value of the program comes from the high-caliber staff—great teachers, specialists

Table 6.1

Cost comparison of in-district and out-of-district severe-needs programs

	Out-of-district	In-district
Number of students served	3	3
Tuition	$50,000 per child	
Transportation	$15,000 per child	
Teacher, with benefits		$75,000
Aides, with benefits		$25,000
Specialized services		$20,000
Transportation		$5,000
Total	$195,000	$125,000
Cost per student	$65,000	$41,667

in autism or behavior disorders, paraprofessionals who provide extra help, and lots of support services staff like counselors and speech therapists. A school district can hire these same people at the same salary, maintain the same student-to-staff ratio for every student, provide the exact same quality of service, and still save nearly 40 percent per student!

While students benefit from great staff, much of the costs are not staff related. Transportation, facilities, and marketing are all sources of savings. From my research, I've found that districts spend about $15,000 on average per student to bus him to an out-of-district placement, but it often costs just a few thousand dollars to bring him into a similar in-district program.

Most out-of-district placements have magnificent facilities; some look more like college campuses than schools. One such out-of-district placement serves just 150 elementary students but has a separate athletics facility, arts center, and dining hall. It, of course, also has to pay for custodial staff, insurance, snow plowing, and other maintenance costs. If each school in a district added just one classroom for four to eight special-needs students, it would not add a single custodian, and all the other building-related costs are also fixed.

Finally, out-of-district placements often spend relatively large sums on marketing efforts, from glossy brochures to staff members devoted to showing prospective parents around. A district can often offer the same program for 40 percent less, saving $25,000 or more per student. The student also gains from being part of his community, enjoying a shorter ride to school, and having a chance to socialize with nondisabled peers.

One midsized district with about six thousand students put this concept into practice and reaped big benefits for students and the budget. With special education costs skyrocketing to 21.4 percent of the total school budget, the district sought to enhance its capacity to educate students with severe special needs in-district—and thereby reduce the need for expensive out-of-district placements—by expanding and adding several special education programs.

Emphasizing services for children with autism and emotional disabilities, the district's program expenditures primarily centered on hiring new teachers, teacher assistants, and speech and language specialists, along with providing related training, supplies, and benefits. However, despite these expenses, the district's new and expanded services significantly reduced out-of-district placements, generating more than $1.3 million in net savings during the first year the programs opened! These savings continued each subsequent year, and over the next few years the district rolled out additional programs and lowered costs even further. These savings allowed the district to navigate the current fiscal crisis relatively unscathed.

Where There's a Will, There's a Room

A large urban district of about fifty thousand students launched a similar effort to serve more special-needs students in-district and saved over $28,000,000 a year! Sounds good, but some districts argue, "We don't have the room for these new classes. We would if we could, but space is the problem." Lack of space is the most common reason that other districts don't follow the lead of these forward-thinking districts, but this obstacle should be confronted.

Let's size the challenge. A district with five thousand students might want to cut its out-of-district placements in half—say, from one hundred students to fifty, thus saving $1,000,000 every year and helping reintegrate fifty kids into the community. If each classroom serves about six students, then only one room needs to be freed up in each of the district's eight schools. Seems possible.

Despite this modest space need, many principals will say with sincerity that they just don't have an extra room. On one level, they are right. Every room is being used, so a quick look confirms that there's no extra space. But, sometimes, they don't *want* to find the space. These programs add demanding parents and needy students to a school's already full plate. There isn't much incentive to find a room.

As superintendent, when I expanded in-district capabilities, I got the same reaction at first, but then I tried to reverse the incentives. Each new program would have a dedicated administrator to interface with parents so the principal wouldn't be the primary contact, and each specialist assigned to the new programs—such as a social worker or an autism expert—would be staffed to provide an hour a day of help to the whole school, not just the new program. These inducements provided enough upside such that some principles suddenly found space where none existed before.

I still needed more space, so I tried something a bit underhanded. I announced to the principals that the school board was considering expanding our very popular gifted and talented program at a few schools. There was a catch, though: it required a dedicated classroom. To be a candidate for housing the new gifted and talented program, each principal had one week to find the space. Within forty-eight hours, *every school freed up a classroom*. One school combined two computer labs into one, moving some computers into the library. Another school had added a second faculty lunchroom, just because it had the extra space,

A CRAZY IDEA?

Pay the Parents

It is jaw-dropping that many districts spend, on average, $15,000 a year to transport students with special needs to out-of-district placements. It is not uncommon to spend $25,000–$30,000 for some students, often transporting a single student in a car. There are many reasons for the high cost, one of which is that each car and driver can only make one run in the morning and one in the afternoon, because all school days start and stop at about the same time. This means a district pays for a full-day driver and car, even though they're only used for a few hours a day. Additionally, some districts provide an aide in the car in addition to the driver. The simple, not-so-crazy idea is to pair up students. Two students in a car travel for the same cost as one. Districts have saved up to 30 percent by teaming with five or six neighboring districts to pool students and routes.

A crazier idea is to pay parents to drive their own children. Some districts offer the standard IRS reimbursements of about 50 cents a mile, but that's not much of an incentive. For a twenty-mile, forty-five-minute trip, the parents would receive $10 a day, or $1,800 a year. When the parents say, "No, thanks, you drive my child; it's the law," the district pays $15,000 a year. What if the district offered mom or dad $7,500 a year? This comes to about $15 an hour, which rivals working retail or many other part-time jobs. In my conversations with parents, some indicated that they would cut back on their part-time work if they could get paid the same or better to be with their child more. Many parents, special education and general education alike, greatly value the quality time of being alone and uninterrupted with their child on the way to school and back.

Parents in one focus group testing interest in the idea took the concept to a bold new level: allow (and facilitate) parents to create car pools. Imagine three families agreeing to carpool. Each receives $7,500 a year, but only has to drive every third day! This seems like a true win-win: a 50 percent savings for the district and happy parents. Some districts, however, might only see the problems. Parents cannot drive other children per district policy. "Liability!" screams the attorney. "Not our job to facilitate carpooling," says the transportation manager. For all the reasons it can't work, it's worth remembering that a great many private schools already do this. At some private day schools, the majority of parents self-organize car pools, taking into account parent work schedules and various afterschool activities. The school makes phone numbers and addresses available on an opt-in basis.

and another school realized that its ELL room was used two hours a day, and its reading room was also just used two hours a day, so they could be shared. One more school announced that a classroom had been converted to a storeroom, which just held unused stuff. And on it went. These spaces housed our new special education programs!

Change the Organizational Structure

The last option for making special education dollars go further is to change who manages the department. Managing special education isn't easy. The laws are tricky, the cost drivers complex, and the financial savings seldom obvious. In most districts, this multidimensional challenge is handed to the special education director or director of pupil services. It is unreasonable to expect one person to oversee:

- Legal and compliance issues
- Programming for students with severe needs
- Teaching and learning strategy
- Budget and financial management

Most districts have a similar chain of command and roles and responsibilities. Unfortunately, the standard arrangement asks a lot of the special education office that goes well beyond its training.

- The special education department is tasked with developing curriculum for struggling students, when the math and English departments have more training.
- Special education transportation in smaller districts is often relegated to a special education office secretary, even though it requires hard bargaining and logistical expertise.
- Overseeing obtaining Medicaid reimbursement is often a small, last priority for an overwhelmed special education administrator, who doesn't have the time to maximize revenue.
- Districts with hundreds or even a thousand paraprofessionals often have no one who oversees this large staff, except the special education director.
- The special education director typically manages and negotiates contracts with outside vendors.

A CRAZY IDEA?

Moving from Regional Collaboration to Regional Competition

For as long as there have been students with severe special needs, there have been regional solutions to meeting the needs of children with low-incidence disabilities. Schools for the blind and the deaf came first, followed by state-sponsored collaborates—also known as *educational service centers* (ESCs)—or regional service centers. They go by different names in different states, but they have much in common. Several school districts band together, or are banded together by state mandate, to create and operate a regional collective effort to provide special education programs for students with severe needs. They only charge what it actually costs to provide the programs. The logic is flawless. Each district may not have enough students to support a program on its own, and the collaborative member districts will lend or rent space in their schools to further lower costs. Best of all, they will be nonprofit organizations, ensuring that the needs of children come first. Typically, the member superintendents act as the board of directors to ensure oversight and accountability.

Over time, however, some regional efforts morph from serving their member districts to serving themselves. This is not an indictment of collaboratives, but an acknowledgment of human nature. Typically, the collaborative plays a tiny role for any one district, serving less than 0.5 percent of total enrollment. The superintendents who make up the board of directors are focused on the 99.5 percent of students not attending the collaborative. Moreover, few superintendents have expertise in severe-needs special education, further limiting their engagement. In my experience, most collaboratives are run by committed directors, typically former special education teachers or directors. They care a lot about their kids and their staff. Unlike the superintendents who sit on the board, regional directors tend to stay in their jobs a long time and build close bonds with their staff.

This combination of limited oversight, caring leadership, and cost-plus pricing can lead to some very expensive practices. Just like the school districts they serve, collaboratives can, unintentionally, focus on stability for adults, not the needs of the districts they serve. A few common examples include:

- When member districts in one collaborative no longer needed a preschool autism program because each district had created its own, the collaborative—rather than reducing the collaborative staff no longer required—added those teachers without a role to a vocational program, and the fees for the job training program rose accordingly.
- When a program at a collaborative was chronically underused (one-third of the spots were unfilled year after year), the collaborative made no effort to change the program because tuition was "high enough to cover the extra staff."

- When superintendents have proposed regionalizing special education transportation (remember, 30 percent savings!), numerous collaborative directors have responded with the comment, "It's a lot of work. We would rather stick with what we are already doing."
- In Massachusetts, the attorney general is investigating many instances of excessive salary, cronyism, and conflicts of interest within the state's collaborative leadership.
- In some states, districts are forced to join collaboratives, and the collaboratives can bill any deficit back to their members. When all districts in one such state faced dramatic cutbacks in state funding, the school districts cut their budgets by 15 percent, but their collaborative, which also lost state funding, simply billed its member districts to cover the shortfall rather than trim its own budget.
- Some collaboratives bill large districts for more than the value of the services received because the numerous small districts can outvote the one or two bigger districts.

Despite the drawbacks to the current system, collaboratives can be powerful engines for quality and efficiencies due to their scale, but the incentives need to be realigned. The need to lower costs while expanding services must outweigh the desire to maintain stability and care for the staff. A six-step reform process might help:

1. **Require each collaborative to publish actual fully loaded costs per student served in each program.** This allows districts to compare and assess cost-effectiveness. In my experience, many collaboratives use accounting practices with more twists and turns than Enron to show low per-pupil costs, while shifting millions of dollars off the books or out of the programs. Strangely enough, many collaboratives only publish their planned costs, not their actual costs.
2. **Encourage collaboratives to compete for district members and students.** Membership is seldom a choice. History, geography, or legislation determines which districts use which collaboratives. This near-monopoly discourages innovation and tough decisions.
3. **Fund collaboratives based on utilization by districts.** If a district doesn't see a need to use a collaborative's services, it

shouldn't pay a penny. Many collaboratives charge annual membership fees, which delinks usage and payment. Having to attract paying customers would shrink or eliminate organizations that don't deliver value.

4. **Instill entrepreneurship in the leadership of collaboratives and regional centers.** Districts could use recruiting practices to target a different type of leader. Some people like to grow an organization. In my experience, some of today's collaborative leaders, who are retired district leaders at the end of their careers, long for simpler times rather than proactively seek change as an exciting challenge.

5. **Create rewards for improved cost-effectiveness.** This means doing the same or better for less and not lowering the quality or services. Leaders of the organization could be compensated based on savings delivered to members. Medicare and Medicaid now tie reimbursements to patient outcomes. Currently, the higher a collaborative's cost structure, the higher its reimbursement.

6. **Absent competition, limit employee benefits and compensation to the average of the districts served.** For example, employee health-care contributions are often less at collaboratives than in the school districts they serve. In some cases, collaborative staff members get the best of what each member district offers its employees. If district A offers great health insurance, the collaborative matches district A. If district B has the best sick-time policy, the collaborative matches district B, and on it goes.

Special education is often a walled fortress, isolated from curriculum leaders, principals, and even superintendents. Students and the budget both suffer. Superintendents, on the other hand, rely extensively on a team to manage their districts. The CFO helps with finances, the director of curriculum assists with teaching and learning, and the accountability staff crunches the achievement numbers. Most special education directors are given much less support and are expected to manage all these functions by themselves, or with limited staff who may not have the same specialized expertise; for example:

- Many CFOs stay away from the special education budget. They provide little or no direction or assistance. Instead, the special education director, aided by clerks and secretaries in midsized districts, often builds the budget.
- Many business and transportation offices provide services for general education, but not special education. It is not uncommon for the regular yellow school buses to be managed by a seasoned transportation director, while the costlier and more complex special education transportation is handled by a secretary or an administrator with a special education, rather than transportation, background.
- Secretaries in the special education central office, not business office staff, also often handle special education vendors and subcontractors, which would never be allowed for "regular" expenses.
- Special education directors seldom get much assistance from curriculum directors, math or English department heads, or reading directors. All teaching and learning falls to them, despite often having no formal training in math, English, reading, or curriculum development.

All too often, when a superintendent gives the annual state-test-scores presentation to the school board, if students with special needs did poorly in math, all heads turn to the special education director and ask, "What are *you* going to do about this?" Why don't the heads turn instead to the director of math, the office of accountability, or the chief academic officer?

Increasing effectiveness and cost-effectiveness in special education needs to be a group effort, with tasks assigned to staff with relevant training and background. A new organizational chart can help:

- *Special education directors* should oversee compliance issues and program development for students with severe special needs.
- *Curriculum leaders and department heads* should oversee teaching and learning for all students, including students with special needs. Staff teaching math, for example, including special educa-

tion teachers, should report to the math department. This would also facilitate better scheduling and staffing, since it would be easier to move positions between general education and special education staffing as needed.

- *The business office* should manage contracts, budgeting, subcontractors, grants, and other financial matters. Sure, it will need lots of cooperation from the special education department, but we shouldn't expect former special education teachers to be business managers any more than we expect CFOs to be experts in special education.

- *The HR office* should manage staffing, scheduling, and building assignments. It does this for all general education staff, but often not for special education teachers. In one district, HR handled the paperwork, notifications, and bumping for all staff during a large-scale layoff—the first in years—except for special education teachers. The special education director was left to navigate the contractual minefield alone and struggled on her own.

Reducing special education costs while raising student achievement is possible, but not easy. Only by assembling the right team with the right mix of skills, and armed with very detailed data, can these opportunities become a reality. The irony is that while many feel that special education costs are uncontrollable, experience has shown that these costs represent one of the most significant areas for savings and increased student learning.

Ten Best Opportunities to Reduce Special Education Costs While Improving Student Outcomes

1. Track the time that special education teachers and therapists spend instructing students. You might be surprised.
2. Review the service delivery model for providing academic support. Some models require three times as many teachers, with no added learning.
3. Increase student independence by reducing paraprofessional support when appropriate.
4. Create clear criteria for entry into special education. Don't confuse insufficient learning with a disability.
5. Create clear exit criteria for special-needs services. Success means that services are no longer required.
6. Provide intensive general education supports, especially in reading.
7. Ensure that general education curriculum leaders manage and monitor the achievement of students with special needs.
8. Create detailed staff schedules and allocate to schools based on student needs.
9. Create a system to measure and manage special education costs led by the business office.
10. Serve more students with severe needs in-district.

7

Technology to the Rescue?

HARNESSING THE
UNTAPPED POTENTIAL

Will online learning bend the cost curve of K–12 education? It might. The Web, iPads, and even cell phones may reshape education, or they might just dig a deeper hole in school budgets.

This is a downer of a chapter. While school budgets are seldom an up-lifting topic, *Smarter Budgets, Smarter Schools* focuses on solutions. I have never cared much for books that describe the problem in detail but don't offer much in the way of advice for beating the challenge. Unfortu-nately, technology as a way to increase learning and decrease costs isn't yet a tale of success, but it ought to be.

Bill Gates and Steve Jobs gave birth to a productivity boom on par with the invention of the wheel and the Industrial Revolution. Just think how much faster word processing is than typing on a Selectric, or how much less expensive it is to view a product on Amazon.com than to get a catalog through the mail. Thanks to Intel, I haven't talked to a bank teller in years. Technology has changed nearly every aspect of how we work and live. In most instances, it has lowered costs and improved outcomes as well.

Technology in the public schools is a different matter. A *Time* cover story on education in the twenty-first century opens with the following:

> There's a dark little joke exchanged by educators with a dissident streak: Rip Van Winkle awakens in the 21st century after a hundred-year snooze and is, of course, utterly bewildered by what he sees. Men and women dash about, talking to small metal devices pinned to their ears. Young people sit at home on sofas, moving miniature athletes around on electronic screens. Older folk defy death and disability with metronomes in their chests and with hips made of metal and plastic. Airports, hospitals, shopping malls—every place Rip goes just baffles him. But when he finally walks into a schoolroom, the old man knows exactly where he is. "This is a school," he declares. "We used to have these back in 1906. Only now the blackboards are green."[1]

This was obviously written before funding from the American Recovery and Reinvestment Act of 2009 (ARRA) forced a zillion smartboards into classrooms across the country, because the boards are all white now. But the basic point is still true: schools haven't yet fundamentally changed the way students are educated—change on the scale of self-serve gas eliminating the pump attendant, Orbitz pushing aside the travel agent, or WebMD replacing a visit to the doctor's office.

New Technologies Need New Structures

The cost of educating a student has steadily risen, even adjusting for inflation. Per-pupil, inflation-adjusted expenditures have risen from about $6,800 to more than $12,600 over the past twenty-five years. Figure 7.1 shows the unhalting rise.

In many industries, technology has fundamentally altered the basic cost equation. Very sophisticated logistics has reduced the cost of air travel and overnight mail, computer-aided design has dropped the cost of the cars we drive, and massive databases and real-time inventory control has allowed big-box retailers to sell us toothpaste and TVs for less.

Based on my experiences with districts across the country, however, it seems that technology has actually *increased* the cost of educating a student, not reduced it. This is primarily because schools have tried to fit new technology into an old mold, rather than allow the tools to redesign

Figure 7.1

Per-pupil total elementary and secondary school expenditures (constant 2009 $)

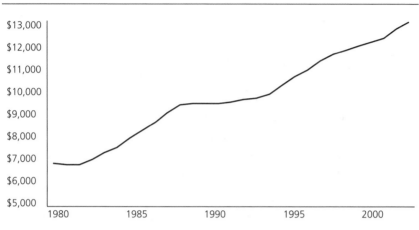

Source: National Digest of Education Statistics.

the system. The following sections detail two compelling and far too common examples.

Online Instruction in an Offline Setting

A hypothetical district wanted to embrace online learning for high school students who didn't function well in a large, socially complex, rule-ridden high school. The idea was to allow these students, many of whom were very bright, to take online classes, perhaps college-level classes. Some top schools and institutions have offered their online classes for free. This seems like a potential win-win—more learning at a much lower cost. Students in this district would take courses from home when they wanted to (typically from 9 p.m. to 2 a.m.) and be monitored and assessed periodically by a teacher.

Good for the student and good for the budget. The average per-pupil cost of educating a student is about $12,000 a year, and the marginal cost (just the teacher salary and materials) is about $3,500 if no extra help is given. This online effort might cost less than $1,000 per student. So how did it all play out?

First, the district bought twenty computers, and then it outfitted a computer lab with tables, special lighting, and air conditioning, despite the fact that all the students owned a computer (or two!). Then a teacher was assigned full-time to the online teaching room, and no more than twenty students were scheduled into each of the five periods of the day. Students were expected to report to the online room per their schedule. Finally, the district purchased a special curriculum. In the best of cases, the cost would have been 50 percent more than traditional education, but in the end, it was more than double the cost, because few students actually showed up to class. How did this happen?

The guidance department insisted that if the students didn't have a fixed schedule, the online learning initiative would be considered home schooling, and the district didn't support home schooling. The department heads were uncomfortable with free courses, and the principal thought a teacher should be assigned if kids were going to get course credit. As crazy as this seems, I have visited many similar "online" classrooms where class size is purposefully kept small, with one teacher, two aides, and a price tag per student three or four times as much as traditional education.

There are so many variations on this theme. One school purchased Rosetta Stone, a self-taught foreign language software program, and then assigned a full-time foreign language teacher to monitor the students while they studied. It didn't matter that it was an independent, self-paced program and that the teachers might not even speak the language being learned.

Maybe all this teacher support, small classes, and fixed schedules are needed for kids to learn. Here's the catch: in these same schools, when the online learning isn't *replacing* an existing class, it is handled very differently. Take, for example, schools that have never offered Italian or art history. They allow students to take these classes online for credit, but without additional adult support. They are never assigned to a classroom or even a class period. It is actual independent study—and it's free. The same is true of students with medical needs. If they are homebound, they take online courses without a teacher, but when they return to school, the district wouldn't give them credit for the same online course. In an era of standards-based education, it seems that if a student can take a course online and get a decent grade on the final exam, then we know she mastered the course material. This doesn't fit, however, the old model of a school requiring a teacher at the front of the room.

Online instruction is only the latest example of schools struggling to increase learning and reduce costs through technology. Sadly, many of the most widely adopted practices actually raise costs and reduce learning. Like many tragedies, our next example starts with love.

Computer Hardware Is Alluring, but at What Price?

In my experience, too many school boards and curriculum leaders fall head over heels for computer hardware. CPUs and iPads are beautiful sirens, calling from the rocky shore. During the 1990s and early 2000s, many schools embraced with vigor an obsession with PCs. I have read strategic plans that called for four computers per classroom. The plans even specified how much RAM each should have. They did not, however, say what a class of twenty-four students should do with four computers. Most striking was that these districts had no numeric goals for kids reading on grade level, or graduating, just for how many computers would be in their classrooms.

I was on the school board of one such smitten district during the PC boom. Budget requests for teacher coaches, mentors, and a curriculum director were considered excessive, but PCs were a necessity. The crowd-out effect went beyond just the budget. The district postponed for a year the planned professional development in math, and replaced it with instruction on how to use the new computers instead. Strangest of all, the computers were almost never used. I would walk the schools, visiting every classroom and counting how many screens were on. Many days it was zero, and never more than a handful. The ultimate insult to injury came when the school board was asked to include dust protectors with each new computer purchased, because a thick layer of crud was building up on the screens and keyboards from disuse.

The problem was, we bought machines but didn't make a plan. No one said, "Our kids are struggling in math, and some teachers struggle to explain math concepts visually, and *Math Made Visual* software [I just made up the name] will address this need for some students. We will need computers to run this program." Instead, we just bought the boxes and hoped for the best.

The most expensive example of using new technology in the old model is the sad story of the lowly overhead projector. Long a fixture in most classrooms, this sturdy, rugged workhorse cost about $200 and seemed to last forever. Sure, the screen got hot, but it worked well. In school after school, I have seen the tide of progress wash away this antiquated solution for projecting information to the whole class. In its place, districts have outfitted classrooms with laptops connected to overhead LCD projectors and smartboards at a cost of about $9,000 in hardware alone. The actual cost is much greater when you include wiring, maintenance, and support. It seems to me that many districts that had unspent ARRA funds bought smartboards first, and hoped to figure out why later.

One would hope that at ten times the cost, there would be ten times the benefit. Some teachers make great use of their smartboards—providing interactive, multimedia instruction—but in many hundreds of classrooms I have visited across the country, most of these setups are dark, and the few that are turned on simply display a static Power-Point image, just like the overhead projector or projecting onto a simple whiteboard or TV monitor. I apologize in advance to the handful of tech-savvy teachers who are taking full advantage of this powerful, interactive technology.

I'm certain that iPads for all won't bend the cost curve, and in fact, if twenty-five students with twenty-five iPads walk into class each day with a teacher in front of the room, costs will rise rather than drop.

Collectively, K–12 districts spend a lot on technology. One report estimates that $20 billion will be spent in 2012.[2] Over the last few decades, public schools have spent heavily on classroom technology without commensurate gains in learning. Tom Vander Ark, the former executive director for education at the Bill and Melinda Gates Foundation and an investor in educational technology companies, was asked by the *New York Times* about the effectiveness of technology on raising student achievement. He responded, "The data is pretty weak. It's very difficult when we're pressed to come up with convincing data." When it comes to showing results, he added, "We better put up or shut up."[3]

It's been about thirty years since the Apple II first became popular in public schools, but the way many schools use technology hasn't changed nearly as much as the technology itself has. I recently learned of one district that purchased scores of iPad 2s for teachers. When asked what the teachers would use them for, with a big smile, the director responded, "We are going to look for apps soon!"

The effectiveness and cost-effectiveness of school technology is not a small matter. At current spending levels of about $400 per student, there's a substantial pot of funds that could be redeployed.[4] For example, the same money could hire an additional 250,000 reading teachers or give a $10,000 raise to every elementary classroom and core-subject secondary teacher. To go far out of the box, would offering 500,000 master teachers $50,000 more each year, but using just a whiteboard, have a greater impact on student achievement than all the interactive technology? I'm not sure, but these are the resource allocation questions of the future.

The love affair seems as strong as ever. When I was superintendent, I routinely monitored the use of classroom technology. Fewer than 2 percent of the PCs were turned on each day in most schools, and our smartboards were used even less than that. Despite the limited utility and tight budgets, there was great pressure to maintain our five-year cycle of updating all the PCs in the district. There were a number of years when we laid off teachers but added PCs.

Allocate Hardware Effectively and Cost-Effectively, Not Equally

When a district combines its love of hardware with a value system that prizes equality, a bad situation gets worse. As discussed in chapter 4, many districts feel compelled to treat each school, teacher, or department the same. This plays out as allocating one reading teacher per school, regardless of size, or cutting every program by 1 percent rather than eliminating completely an effort that is no longer aligned with the district's strategy. This definition of equality leads to a lot of extra costs when it comes to technology.

When new schools are built, there is pressure to put a smartboard in every room, including kindergarten, art, and music. Every classroom gets the same number of computers—about four or five. LCD projectors are built into the ceiling of every room in the building. In some schools, only the bathroom is left technology-free. Unfortunately, overspending on underused hardware drains funds from more productive uses.

Provide Technology Only to Those Who Will Use It

There are two alternatives worth considering. The first is to put the technology where it will be used. I remember one tech-comfortable teacher who asked all the other teachers in her grade if she could have their PCs. She had noticed they hadn't been turned on in years. The computer-comfortable teacher embraced technology, but a handful of computers isn't enough for whole-class assignments. She needed at least twelve PCs, enough for half the class, to infuse the tool into core instruction. Happy for the extra space, the nonusers offered up their dusty machines. When the principal learned of the move, the tech-savvy teacher was required to return the PCs to their "rightful owners." It wasn't fair, the principal explained, for one teacher to hoard all of the computers.

Share Fewer Tools Among More Classrooms

I encountered a similar situation when it came to smartboards and LCD projectors. Some classes got them through grants or the PTO. There was pressure to create a five-year capital plan to outfit every room with these seldom-used tools. "All kids deserved equal access," I was told. It seemed more like all teachers deserved equal treatment. My concerns about technology spending were well known, so the administrators took me on a road trip to persuade me. They asked me to see technology in action, which they hoped would move me. I agreed, and asked them to coordinate the class visits with my secretary. When I saw the schedule, I was concerned. The visits were spread over many weeks and never back to back. This seemed wasteful of my time, and disrespectful to the team advocating for the equipment. I asked that we spend one full day the following week and put the discussion to bed either way, but quickly.

Turns out, we couldn't build the schedule that way. Even our most active users only used the interactive portion of the technology once in a while, not every period or even every week, just for key lessons. My mind raced back to my early childhood, when teachers requested the movie projector from the AV department. No one considered putting an expensive projector in every room, but rather a few units were shared across the school. We did the modern-day equivalent. By creating mobile kits composed of a smartboard, PC, and LCD projector, we could serve twenty to thirty classrooms with only three kits. A few teachers were heavy users, and seemed to "own" a set, which was fine. If and when staff members started to fight over availability, we would happily buy more.

It's interesting to compare school use of technology hardware to the private sector. In the business world, everyone has their own computer—no one shares—but smartboards are rare. Even in high-tech companies like software firms, the simple whiteboard is the board of choice. Yes, people often photograph the board with their cell phones, or the boards line every wall, including the hallways, but they don't *interact* with it. LCD projectors are in the ceiling of a conference room or two, but most are portable and moved as needed.

Purchase—and Then Use—Instructional Software Thoughtfully

Districts may like hardware, but they also like software. Like the joy that comes with the birth of a child, I have seen many a curriculum director beam as they talk about their recent software purchases. "We just bought Read 180," they boast, or "We use Study Island!" They quickly start to recite the marketing brochure, "It's interactive. Kids today are digital natives. This will reach them. It has progress monitoring, and adjusts to the child's learning level and style." What I seldom hear, however, is that it helped fifty students get to grade level, that sixty kids made eighteen months of progress in just nine months, or that more kids really understand the concepts of Algebra I.

It seems that *buying* software is exciting and full of promise. *Using* software is a different story. One superintendent learned that millions of dollars of software licenses had never been activated. In another district, hundreds of user seats were purchased, even though only a dozen kids were scheduled for the software-based intervention. One district, back in the day, bought software disks for every PC in the elementary schools, even though only half had enough memory to run them.

The disconnect between buying and actually using software seems to stem from treating software as something different from regular teaching and learning. For example, most districts assemble teams of classroom teachers to write curriculum or pilot a new textbook. Software, however, is often purchased in isolation at the central office level. In some districts, it is the IT director, not even the curriculum director, who makes the selection, but happily this practice is fading. The hallmark of instructional software purchasing, in my experience, is that teachers are much less likely to be involved in developing the statement of need, in piloting and evaluating the options, and in mapping out the implementation. As a result, they are often unclear on its role, unhappy with the functionality, or unsure which children would benefit.

Even when used, instructional software hasn't yet revolutionized teaching and learning. Public schools spent almost $2 billion on classroom software, without a transformation on the scale of how Microsoft Word changed typing or how Orbitz changed booking an airline ticket.[5]

Software Can Enhance Teaching but Does Not Replace It

As you read this chapter, it will be easy to imagine that I don't like or understand technology. As I reread my own words, I picture an old, stuffy guy complaining about people not writing letters anymore and hoping for the return of the Rand McNally atlas in every car and an encyclopedia in every house. I'm not that guy. It is the twentieth-century approach, not twenty-first-century technological advances, that makes this chapter a bit negative so far. I think the potential for fundamental change to K–12 education exists through technology, but many districts have placed too much hope on the devices, while downplaying the role of the teacher and systems thinking.

Just as seldom-used PCs and smartboards can raise expenses without a related increase in learning, poorly planned software purchases can also waste funds and actually reduce student achievement. Too often, we hope software will work miracles and overcome mediocre teaching. The data is clear: nothing matters more than the teacher. Software can be a powerful tool for a talented instructor, but it can't replace teaching or teachers. Just as a sharp set of finely crafted chisels helps a sculptor create a masterpiece, giving just anybody the same set of chisels won't result in anything but cut fingers and stone dust.

I am often asked, "Is Read 180 good?" or "Is Study Island effective?" My answer always seems to disappoint: "It can be." These programs and others have helped many students make tremendous progress. Some foreign language instruction software has helped students gain fluency. In all cases, there was also a good teacher in the mix.

It is common, however, that the software is intended as a substitute for good teaching. One assistant superintendent told me, "Our people struggle with teaching math, so we are buying *XYZ* software," or "We can't afford remediation teachers, so we are buying the software and will have an aide monitor the room." This seldom works. Software like Read 180 and others have some impressive stats. They have been blessed by the What Works Clearinghouse and dozens of independent studies that show it can help children learn to read. But before you run out and buy the product, keep in mind that many, if not most, of the lowest-performing schools in America also use the very same software. I'm confident that Scholastic ships the same product to all of its customers. This difference is *how* it is used, not *what* is used.

Technology Alone Can't Work Miracles

Another cautionary tale of hoping technology will be a workaround for a broken system is the hyper-rise and -fall of some "High-Tech High." One high-profile effort to raise urban achievement in Philadelphia spared no expense. It boasted gleaming laptops for all, smartboards in every nook and cranny, wireless connections everywhere, the backing of Bill Gates, and constant visits by national media. But this futuristic model school was doomed by old obstacles. Maintenance staff didn't run the needed electrical cabling on time, union contracts placed teachers who didn't want to be in this new-fangled school there anyway, and constant turnover of building and district leadership eroded the program's vision. All the technology in the world couldn't overcome this less-than-functional context. Again, the lesson of High-Tech High and Read 180 isn't that technology can't improve the cost-effectiveness of a good school system, but that it can't, by itself, fix a broken one.

Demystify Technology

Another practice that undermines the power of technology in schools is the desire to treat it as different from other teaching tools, even rarified. Many years ago, I read a *Wall Street Journal* editorial on school technology, and it wondered if, in the Middle Ages, when quills became more widespread, schools of the time put them all in one room and had special classes on using them. It seems silly, but the computer lab and the technology teacher are a close analogy. In many schools I visit today—fewer each year, happily—technology is a separate subject rather than a tool to improve teaching and learning of math, English, art, etc.

Just a few years ago, and maybe still happening today, I visited a middle school that was very proud of its technology integration efforts. So proud, it had a technology department and staff and required courses. All students learned how to use PowerPoint, for example, during sixth-grade technology class. Unfortunately, most students in this middle-class district had been using PowerPoint at home since they were first-graders. Worse yet, they didn't use PowerPoint in English. They wrote papers; they didn't create presentations or present verbally to their class—the very purpose of PowerPoint.

Technology seems too often to be locked up like a rare manuscript. My college was proud of its collection of gilded illuminated texts. They were locked up, and only a special librarian had access to them. In schools, we sometimes lock up and mystify instructional technology as well. Take the Kurzweil machine. This useful device reads text to students who struggle. Many districts keep it in the "Kurzweil room," where the one teacher trained in using it places a book onto the platen and hits go. Students are almost always pulled out of class to "get Kurzweil" as if it's a special treatment. Worse, there is often only one highly trained special education teacher, or even more highly trained Adaptive Technology teacher (yes, there is such a position), sitting with just one student at a time. The irony is, nearly every Windows-based computer has this text-to-speech function built into the software for free, and the student can surely text a zillion words a minute while simultaneously tweeting and scanning his Facebook wall, so why couldn't he instead stay in class, plug some earbuds into his PC, and listen to the textbook?

I have seen this "technology is too special for regular people to use" attitude pushed to the extreme. One teacher, who wanted her fifth-graders' biography speeches filmed (picture Johnny dressed up as Lincoln, telling his life story), requested that the technology integration teacher come videotape the class because no one else was trained on the equipment. This was a handheld camera, the stuff of home movies—just point and shoot.

There is no doubt that many teachers are comfortable with technology and use it on their own. Every year, I see more of this, but it still seems like technology being used for technology's sake, not for the sake of enhancing learning. One teacher I know took the initiative to move her ELA lessons into the twenty-first century. She scanned her worksheets as PDFs, loaded them onto the computers in the computer room, and marched her kids to the lab to type in the fill-in-the-blank answers rather than write them in pencil. Of course, a computer lab tech "needed" to be present to help keep the printers running and handle any crashes. Another teacher, determined to embed technology into her foreign language class, got a grant to buy iPods and assigned all students to record their speaking assignment and download it. This was podcasting, and very high tech—unfortunately, it was no different from our language lab, which already recorded students talking.

Technology can improve teaching and learning, and it can be cost-effective as well. The steps outlined in "Ten Ideas to Consider Before Purchasing New Technology" can help ensure that students and the budget both benefit.

Ten Ideas to Consider Before Purchasing New Technology

1. Start by identifying a teaching and learning need to be filled, rather than focusing on the technology itself.
2. Don't tie technology to a room—let it move where and when needed.
3. Create from the outset a means to measure whether the new technology is raising student achievement.
4. Start with volunteers. Not all staff may want the new technology.
5. Ask which policies, practices, or schedules must change to take full advantage of the new technology.
6. Value administrative technology as much as classroom technology.
7. If significant professional development is required, then perhaps some staff members aren't ready for the new technology.
8. Calculate the total cost to educate a student before and after the adoption of the new technology. Technology should lower costs, not raise them.
9. Consider utilizing student-owned technology before purchasing for the district.
10. Remember, good teaching still matters most.

Maximize Technology's Potential to Enhance Teacher Effectiveness

On the whole, many districts have purchased a lot of technology that hasn't led to learning gains, but they have as a consequence shifted a great many resources away from reading, coaching, and other less exciting expenses. If districts just stopped unproductive practices, the budget situation would improve without a loss of learning. Despite the net negative impact of some past technology decisions, technology does have the potential to transform both the cost and quality of K–12 education.

Few people know more about both technology and education than Bill Gates. He became the world's richest man by shaping the Information Age and now is putting his fortune toward improving public education through the Bill and Melinda Gates Foundation, which is the largest education philanthropy in the country. A quick review of the Foundation's current efforts helps keep the role of technology in perspective. Its major initiatives focus on teacher effectiveness, high national standards, teacher evaluation, charter schools, and the use of data. All could be accomplished with pencil, paper, typewriters, or mimeographs.

While technology can speed and support these important efforts, it does not replace them. Technology isn't the solution; it's a tool to implement flesh-and-blood strategies. Nothing matters more at the school or district level to student achievement than the quality of the teacher. Nothing impacts per-pupil costs more than the number of students taught by each teacher. So can technology improve both the quality of teaching and the number of students taught by great teachers? Many think the answer is yes.

Use Technology to Aid Struggling Students

Simple technology could greatly help some struggling students, many with special needs. The quintessential middle or high school classroom includes the daily ritual of teacher talks, teacher writes on the whiteboard, kids listen, and kids take notes. This works for most students, but not all. Some can't listen and write; others can't listen and process quickly. This is a classic challenge for students with high-functioning Asperger's syndrome, but it is also common with many students who eventually drop out. Power-Point can be the difference between an F and a B. I have observed some very organized teachers prepare what goes on the board in PowerPoint form and project the slides onto the whiteboard. In one such class, a student had an IEP that called for a scribe, a full-time person to take notes for the child. The teacher, not wanting another adult in the room, and believing the student was distracted by the aide, just printed a copy of the slides for the student. In time, other kids asked for the notes, and soon everyone got them. Most kids still take notes in class, but then double-check them at home against the PowerPoint slides. Others found that listening alone was best, and the notes could supplement their memory later. To save on paper, the notes could be posted online.

Move Training and Professional Development Online

Another simple way to enhance teacher effectiveness may be through online professional development. Most PD is an hour or two of someone smart talking to a group of teachers. Research from Learning Forward (formerly the National Staff Development Council) says fifty hours of training on a given subject is needed to change behavior. Web-based training can help. Both the Knowledge Is Power Program (KIPP) and the Harvard Business School, for example, support new staff via online training. A practitioner explains the strategy, and then an in-class example is available for viewing. The demonstration helps people see the point more clearly. Being able to watch from home, rather than attending afterschool sessions, also makes it more likely that many more hours on the same subject can be covered during the course of a year. Perhaps best of all, if one person, district, or company produced great video instruction, thousands or millions of teachers could watch at little added cost.

Record Actual Instruction to Provide Better Teacher Feedback

Filming teachers at work and providing feedback takes the video idea to the next level. The needed technology has been cheap and easy since the day of the Betamax, but very few teachers are routinely videoed and critiqued. If improving teacher quality is of primary importance, then even a smartphone video recording could dramatically improve the impact of a principal's feedback.

Post Exemplary Lesson Plans Online

Beyond posting training online, districts can leverage the Web to help improve instruction by posting effective lesson plans as well. This should not be confused with the many wikis that have popped up, where teachers upload and download their favorite materials. One very excited and generous teacher I know spent three weekends uploading her lesson plans, handouts, and assessments. The problem was, student data suggested she was an ineffective teacher. Free stuff is sometimes worth what you pay for it. There are two ways to make sharing effective. KIPP uploads material only from teachers who have proven to be effective. It's an honor, not a birthright, to be included.

A more democratic alternative is the Epicurious model. The cooking magazine allows many to post recipes, but an active user base reviews and mercilessly critiques them. If people read ten comments that say the soup was too salty, few will download the post.

Use Technology as a Diagnostic Tool for Targeted Instruction

Online PD can be less expensive than in person, but districts don't actually spend a lot of money on teacher training, so it's not a huge financial driver. Districts do spend a lot on remediation and intervention, however—reading teachers, aides, special education teachers, afterschool programs, extended days, not to mention the social cost of students dropping out. Technology can help struggling students in two ways, but not necessarily the common approach of buying a computer program to provide the supplemental instruction. Struggling students need targeted intervention and talented, effective teachers.

Kids who struggle in, say, geometry don't necessarily struggle in every way, shape, and form. Is the root issue with number sense, the concept of fractions, the logic flow of proofs, or memorization of the formulas to calculate area? We don't expect a doctor's stethoscope to cure us when we are sick, but it does help him figure out what *he* can do to help. In the same way, software can be a powerful diagnostic tool to identify specific areas of need.

Personalize the Instruction

Once the topic of concern is pinpointed, a talented teacher will know what to focus on. An interesting question is, "Does this instructor need to be in the same room as the student?" Most of us can remember that one amazing teacher who made a subject seem so easy to understand. As a superintendent, I wished every student in my district could learn math from Mr. Hannigan, my high school hero who made math engaging and crystal-clear.

Mr. Hannigan has long since retired, but there is Patrick Jones, an instructor at Vanderbilt University with a talent for explaining math. His YouTube tutorials, Patrick JMT (short for Patrick Jones math tutoring), reteach hundreds of mini-lessons, down to the fine level of detail that some students need. This free site has been accessed by 17 million users over the last three years. I learned about the site while expressing my displeasure to my son, who had decided to no longer attend the afterschool math help sessions at school. With a Cheshire cat's grin, he told me he no longer *needed* to stay after school to receive tutoring. With a "you are so old and out-of-date, so twentieth century" tone in his voice, he introduced me to Patrick Jones. My son had switched because, as he put it, Jones "is a better teacher, at least for my learning style, and I don't have to listen to the stuff I already know and can focus instead on my trouble areas." I was glad for my son, but felt a bit silly. Like many districts, we actually block YouTube at the high school rather than encourage it.

In under a minute, my son had introduced me to *personalized learning*. More than just a collection of video clips, personalized learning is the idea that certain approaches work best with certain students and that each child starts with a different foundation of skills, struggles in selected areas, and takes a different amount of time to learn a subject. Any teacher will say, "Duh! *All* kids are different." Unfortunately, many schools structure teaching and learning as if all kids are the same.

Students are typically assigned to subject by year of birth (all ninth-graders take geometry), we assign students randomly to teachers (they are all highly qualified), and most everyone gets the same material one hour a day for 180 days. Our response to the obvious fact that students learn differently is to ask teachers to differentiate their instruction, but still hold constant the lesson plan, content, and time. Technology might change this.

Imagine students being assessed at the start of the school year and profiled based on their learning style. What if they were taught just the content they didn't already know and were paired with a teacher who taught in their learning style? Technically, you could do this without technology, but software diagnostics, some online instruction, and targeted computer-generated practice work—all supported by in-person teaching—make it easier to pull off personalized learning. In this scenario, some students might spend three days on chapter one, some three weeks, and some might jump straight to chapter two. Moreover, grade levels don't start in September and end in June. Students could move to the next topic when ready. The role of the teacher is still critical, but different. The teacher would provide some core instruction and lots of mini-lessons, but fewer would be with the whole class. As strange as this might sound to a high school teacher, it is exactly what most elementary teachers do when using the writers and readers workshop model, which is widely accepted across the country.

Personalized learning could have incredible advantages for English language learners (ELLs). Today, we (figuratively) ask for a birth certificate to create a student's course schedule. If born in 1999, a student from Honduras is assigned to seventh-grade math, English, science, social studies, plus an ELL class. What if the student never took math before? Wouldn't it be more effective to focus on the skills in sequential order rather than assuming that every twelve-year-old from Honduras should be on seventh-grade level and must have had the same math as kids who have lived in town for the last six years? Even ELL instruction could benefit from targeted, individual instruction based on need and interest.

Gifted students will also benefit from more flexible learning. A student who masters fifth-grade math by January is doomed to boredom as the class moves forward at a pace suitable to the average student. A more online, mastery-based approach would allow so-called sixth-grade math to start whenever a student is ready.

Try Distance and Online Learning

The biggest, boldest idea for technology to transform the cost and quality of education is *distance learning*. The concept is simple, but still unproven. Currently, nearly all instruction takes place with one teacher in front of approximately twenty-five students for most of the day, and even fewer students in the room during remediation and intervention classes. It's just a given that the teacher drives to school each morning and the kids get bused to the same building at the same time.

As a *Star Trek* fan growing up, I often wished for a transporter. This futuristic device, of "Beam me up, Scotty" fame, had just three simple levers and quickly moved people thousands of miles. It's not as cool, but Skype comes close. I routinely talk to clients and my children away at college through this free videoconferencing service. The *Chronicle of*

Higher Education reported a story that a student called his professor (likely on a smartphone), saying he was snowed in and asking whether could he attend class via Skype. The professor placed a laptop with a webcam on a desk, and the student not only virtually attended class, but he even gave a five-minute presentation.[6]

This worked for the one weather-bound student. What if the professor was outstanding, like Mr. Hannigan or Patrick Jones? Might fifty kids remotely attend this lesson? Or a thousand? How far can we leverage the talents of one great teacher? Could we video the teacher and let ten thousand people watch on their own schedule? But when does this stop being teaching and morph into just watching TV or a movie? Watching a NOVA series on the formation of the Earth doesn't replace a course on Earth science.

The economics of online learning are straightforward. Today, a typical secondary core-subject teacher works with about 125 students (five periods a day, each with 25 students in the class), and remediation teachers work with far fewer students, often about 15–40 per year. If online learning allowed each of these teachers to support twice as many students, then districts would need half as many of these teachers. Not all positions would be cut in half; you still need the same number of principals, nurses, PE teachers, etc. If middle schools and high schools, but not elementary schools, used technology to double the average teaching load, then an individual district of five thousand students would free up more than $3.5 million a year, and a district of fifty thousand would be able to reallocate almost $40 million, which scales to estimated savings of $35 billion a year nationwide.

This makes the billion-dollar question, "How do you provide a top-quality education that requires only half as many teachers at the secondary level?" Unfortunately, we don't have a good recipe yet, but we might know the ingredients. Imagine a much more nuanced use of technology and class size. As an example, we'll use a single math class, a subject that tends to already have a lot of "extra help" teachers:

Monday: Fifty students hear a lecture overviewing the key concepts.
Tuesday: Some students work independently, viewing online material and taking online assessments. They also "chat" through threaded

discussions with their teacher (think e-mailing back and forth). Other students work with tutorial software to identify their areas of weakness and their preferred learning styles.

Wednesday: The fifty students meet for half a period. The teacher presents an explanation of the most common questions raised through the threaded discussion. Struggling students spend the remainder of the period working with in-person remediation teachers.

Thursday: Some students work independently with online content, practice exercises, and assessments. Others work with both online and small-group support. In both cases, an online assessment gauges what they've mastered in the past week.

Friday: All fifty students attend class. Both the core and remediation teacher work in small groups focusing on specific skills gaps.

The scenario for a course in social studies might be even simpler. A class of twenty-five students meets every other day with their teacher. On the off days, they work independently with online instructors, engage in threaded discussions with their peers, take online tours of relevant locales, and write research papers. The online instruction could be a combination of prerecorded videos and live lectures shared by thousands of students at once. One of the most appealing aspects of this model is that students could select topics, within a certain range, that interest them. For example, a typical US history course discussing the Great Depression will touch on a number of causes and impacts, but the online self-directed portion could allow one student to focus more deeply on the role of stock-market speculation, and another to delve into the impact on women in society at the time. The key higher-order learning skills can be mastered regardless of content focus. A flesh and blood teacher can't offer such variety.

Both the math and the social studies examples require half as many teachers and hold the promise of more learning and increased engagement. Yes, a promise, but not a reality. Districts need to experiment to determine the right mix of each element for a given type of student. Current technology is sufficient and widely used, but typically all bets are placed on just one element. A thoughtful combination of live instruction, Skype lectures, online video, web-based tours, texting-based group discussion, software-generated tutorials, targeted video remedial instruction, and frequent assessment are all likely needed. Given the upside in learning and savings, it's worth the effort to experiment.

This concept is already used by the Rocketship Education, a hybrid charter school network, which includes one self-taught period a day, thus reducing required teacher staffing by 20 percent.

One of the side effects of distance learning is that school facilities could shrink. Less classroom space is needed, and some students could even work at home some of the time as an earned privilege. *Hybrid learning*, the combination of in-person and online instruction, is the big, bold futuristic bet for technology in our schools, but there is an equally powerful (but much duller) use for technology that is guaranteed to save money and raise student achievement.

Build a Digital Nervous System: Administrative Technology

Bill Gates, back in 1999 when AOL dialup was still king, shared a vision for technology in schools at the annual American Association of School Administrators (AASA) conference. Gates said he saw a future where school districts would develop strong "digital nervous systems"—electronic systems that provide access to the information and collaboration tools schools need to meet today's instructional and administrative challenges. He further explained that a "digital nervous system can help districts become more efficient, improve strategic decision making, increase parental involvement, and, most important, set the stage for improved student learning."[7]

When one school district in Arizona invested $33 million in laptops, smartboards, and Wi-Fi, it was front-page news. When Broad Prize–winning districts invest heavily in strong data-processing systems, it's just a yawn on the national scene. And when my school board wanted to cut the district's sole data analyst, it was greeted with much enthusiasm. Administrative technology may not be sexy, but it can make a big difference for teachers and students.

Sticking with the model that technology should enhance the delivery of an effective education, but isn't a subject or solution in and of itself, let's recap some key elements of effective districts:

- They use data to inform instruction and intervention. Nearly every school district that has raised student achievement counts data as a key element of success.
- Parent and students are engaged. Administrators and teachers alike plead for more involvement.
- They attract and retain motivated staff.

Relatively low-cost, well-established technology—the stuff that forms a digital nervous system—is often an area of underinvestment, whereas the more visible classroom technology may be overspent.

Automate and Streamline Student Data Tracking and Analysis

It seems odd that, in the world of Twitter, 24/7 news, and next-day shipment on fifty-inch TVs, it takes many districts weeks or months to share with a teacher the results of common formative assessments, the heart of a data-driven school. The data is intended to refine teaching approaches, identify reteaching needs, and group students with like challenges. It's more typical that the teacher has moved on to the next chapter by the time the results are returned and analyzed. Current technology allows some districts to analyze, graph, and share this data in twenty-four hours.

Use a Parent Portal

Many districts already own the technology to dramatically increase parent and student engagement, but they have decided not to use it. Virtually all schools use a student information system to track attendance, create state reports, build schedules, etc. These programs often include a *parent portal* feature. This functionality allows parents and students to monitor attendance, check that homework was turned in, and view grades. It also simplifies communication with teachers. In short, it solves the problem of the "grunt." When parents ask how school was, seemingly every child past third grade grunts, "Fine." When asked if they did their homework, they grunt, "Yes," and when asked how they are doing in math, they grunt, "OK." Then they mumble, "I think."

Parent portals provide more substantial answers. My own experience as a parent of three mirrors many others. Through a parent portal, I learned that my daughter hadn't been eating lunch for weeks, despite getting two bucks every morning; that my son had not turned in a number of assignments he missed while out sick; and that my other son's grades were dropping in English. In all three cases, my wife and I started a conversation and addressed the issues.

If most districts have the parent portal capability, why do so few turn it on? Some teachers seem to fear it or resent it. Even at my children's school, less than half the staff uses it. As superintendent, when I tried to flip the switch, the teacher union leaders resisted greatly, and prevailed. It would have been easier to get $250,000 for new PCs than to share in real time with parents the student progress data that we already had.

Upgrade HR Technology

The last example of underinvestment in administrative technology is the HR department. While some districts have very sophisticated HR systems, I'm surprised by how antiquated many districts remain. In the private sector, HR became fully automated in the 1960s and 1970s, and has been outsourced more recently to even more automated vendors like ADP. Now, even private-sector companies' benefits management is handled online via third-party vendors. In short, it's high-tech, low-cost, and efficient.

Compare this to what I had as superintendent. Paper forms, index cards, and file cabinets on end. Yes, we had computers also, but staff members were listed in multiple databases, none of which tied together. It took days, if not weeks, of manual checking just to get a current list of all staff members and their roles, schedules, and salaries. By the time it was done, things had already changed. The majority of the districts I have worked with also struggle to quickly and accurately manage staffing records. Beyond the inefficiency, this hurts staff morale, a valuable commodity. Rather than help manage people, many HR systems unintentionally frustrate our most important asset: the staff. This includes the panicked call from a newly hired teacher saying she had to take a job elsewhere because she never got her formal offer letter, or the wave of union grievances when the reduction-in-force (layoff) list specified the wrong names because the computer had incorrect seniority dates and certifications.

As I mentioned at the start of the chapter, it is easier to find fault with the current use of technology than to point to dramatic successes. Certainly, many districts have embraced solid administrative uses of technology, and all should. The lack of transformative impact from classroom technology should give us all pause before we push into iPads, virtual schools, or the like. As new tools and techniques evolve, the nuanced application of humans, in combination with a hyperfocus on mastery of knowledge—not coolness of the medium—and a requisite for high academic return on investment, may in fact be the country's best chance to raise achievement while reducing the cost to educate a child.

A CRAZY IDEA?

Pack a Pencil, Notebook, Lunch, and iPad from Home

Nearly all schools expect children to bring their own pencils and notebooks to school. The mad rush at any Staples store in late August is testimony to the quantity of school supplies parents provide. What if we asked parents to provide notebooks—the computer kind, not just the spiral-bound ones? Expanding the question, must schools buy instructional technology, or can they use what students and families already own? I have never been a fan of user fees or parent-subsidized public education, but two experiences brought me to this idea.

Just as school was starting one morning, a short circuit burned out the transformer at a middle school. There would be no power or heat for at least a day. Emergency protocols went into action. Our automated calling system would inform parents and seek permission to send students home or make other arrangements. The problem was, our phone list wasn't easily sorted by school; in addition, we had home phone numbers, but most parents worked. As the adults tried to figure out a plan, the kids stepped into action. Over 98 percent of the students had cell phones, which we ban from class. Students called their parents (also on their cell phones) and, in less than twenty minutes, plans were made for a thousand students and the school emptied out.

Not long after, a frustrated teacher at another school shared with me that her students were bucking her efforts to infuse technology into her instruction. They refused to make videos because our cameras used tape (and thus couldn't be edited with iMovie), and few computers in the library ran the latest version of Flash for animation work. The students asked if they could use their own equipment, which was much better. The teacher said no because it wouldn't be fair to those who didn't have their own equipment. I asked, "How many kids don't have access to the needed equipment?" She didn't know; she never asked. Turns out, in this middle-class community, virtually everyone had better hardware and more modern software at home than what was available at the school. It was easy to form groups for this team project to ensure equal access to cutting-edge home equipment for all. In hindsight, this made perfect sense. Our district policy was to replace our technology over a five- or six-year cycle. Many families upgraded more often.

Nationally, 84 percent of families with school-age children have a computer with Internet access at home as of 2009, and fully 93 percent have access to a home computer.[8] In addition, 75 percent of kids aged twelve to seventeen had a cell phone in 2009 as well.[9] The profile of urban families is slightly different, but for the millions of students not attending urban schools, home technology usually trumps school technology. It's just a guess, but I suspect students own more Kindles and iPads than public schools do.

The cell phone is the most ubiquitous student-owned technology, with wide usage even in urban settings. Generally speaking, my experience has been that schools don't embrace student-owned devices; many districts actually ban them. What if we embraced them instead? Students could photograph the whiteboard to double-check their notes. Shouldn't all students take a snapshot of tonight's homework assignment? Should recording an important lecture on a smartphone be grounds for expulsion (like it was in my district), or encouraged? As web-enabled smartphones become as powerful as the PC of a few years ago, should we continue to block Wi-Fi connections in schools, or incorporate online research into class discussion and tests? It is odd that I can instantly search for a date in history while walking to the hotdog stand near my office for lunch, but I would have expelled a student for doing the same thing during a final.

Like a modern-day Dorothy searching for a way home, we have had the answer with us all along—not the ruby slippers on our feet, but the cell phone in our pocket. I have been pleased by how many teachers and PTOs have wanted "clickers," or student response systems. This system lets kids select A, B, C, or D in multiple-choice fashion to answer questions posed to the class. It is a fast way to check for understanding. Unfortunately, it can cost $2,000 to outfit a classroom, or $250,000 for every class in a large school. Nearly every student, however, already owns a personal response device, also known as cell phone texting. Not only is it free to schools, but students can also send full sentences, not just multiple-choice answers. If we put our minds to it, could we make this a viable class participation tool?

Districts could embrace student-owned technology, but will need to redesign policy, discipline, and rules while ensuring access to the small number of students who don't have the devices. There are plenty of obstacles and legitimate concerns of equity, but finding solutions to these issues could free up funds for other uses while infusing technology into the classroom.

8

A New Approach to Capital Purchases

REINING IN THE COST OF
CONSTRUCTION, RENOVATION, AND
INSTRUCTIONAL MATERIALS

From building new schools and closing old ones to buying textbooks or boilers, school districts spend big dollars on big projects—but not always wisely. New systems and incentives can help.

I thought I would never hear, "It's only $450,000; we should get it, even if we aren't sure we are going to use it." The words "it's only" and "$450,000" don't often get strung together in the same sentence during a school budget meeting. The ultimate irony is that the speaker was the same person who, a few years earlier, held up approval of the district's operating budget because the five VCRs listed in the technology equipment appendix cost $250 each, and they could be purchased for $99, he believed, if the district waited for a sale. A room of thirty school and town leaders, who had debated for thirty minutes whether to cut the technology budget by $750, happily blessed the $450,000 purchase for security cameras in thirty seconds.

Why the inconsistency? One was a capital purchase, and the other was an operating budget expenditure. In my experience, even the most level-headed fiscal conservative can turn into a free spender, like a sailor on shore leave who just got paid after six months out at sea, when it comes to capital spending.

The subject of school capital purchases and construction isn't discussed as often as class size or teacher pensions, so let's start with a few definitions:

A *capital purchase* is technically any item that is expected to last more than three years. In a typical public school district, the largest capital purchases are school buildings, new or renovated. The other common capital purchases include building repairs, technology such as computers and software, textbooks, curriculum materials, and furniture. In short, physical stuff that lasts a while.

The alternative is *operating budget* expenditures. These are typically thought of as the "regular" district budget purchases and include salaries, transportation, minor repairs and maintenance, and the vast majority of what it takes to run a district day in and day out.

Many school boards have a love-hate relationship with capital purchases. I have seen textbook purchases delayed every year for ten years because "we need to keep class sizes small." This mind-set kept social studies teachers in front of twenty-year-old maps that didn't reflect the creation of forty or fifty new countries. On the other hand, building schools can trump all else. I have seen many a new school with gleaming, high-tech libraries and advanced multimedia centers, but no funds for librarians. Smartboards and laptops sail through budget deliberations, but training for math teachers and the math director's salary are cut in exchange. Buying stuff doesn't raise student achievement when compared to having a talented teacher in front of the room. Much research suggests a great teacher in a crummy building with chalk in hand will serve students better than a mediocre teacher with a gleaming smartboard in a sparkling new school. The question is, how do we buy the stuff we need for the least cost so that we can invest the balance in ensuring that every room has an effective teacher?

Capital expenditures, by nature, are very big. The Los Angeles public school system launched a $20 billion capital spending program for new schools, and even a small district with an annual operating budget of just $10 million might have a capital budget of $50 million when it's time for a new school. Even if no new construction is launched, buying a new set of textbooks and related materials in a single subject can easily cost a few hundred dollars per student, which translates to $1 million for a district of five thousand students or $10 million for a system with fifty thousand students.

My life's journey should have prepared me well to deal with capital purchasing when I moved from the private sector to K–12 leadership. For the first half of my professional life, I designed and sold capital equipment, and my product was often part of new or renovated factories. I had participated in over five hundred capital construction projects, working daily with architects, contractors, and the like in dozens of industries in fifty states and on a few continents. I figured this was a decent background to understand capital spending and construction in a school district. Not so!

My experiences suggest that in a world of scarce dollars, capital spending is an area for significant gains without negatively impacting students. I have seen a lot, and not much of it is pretty. Through the years, I volunteered on a building committee charged with overseeing the construction of new schools; as a school board member, I was often asked to approve capital budgets, new schools, additions, and renovations. As superintendent, I wrestled with building new schools or renovating old schools and nixed many capital purchases. Finally, as a consultant, I have watched districts big and small run bond campaigns to fund millions and billions of dollars of construction. The *system* is, by design, one that overspends and underdelivers.

There are many reasons why capital and construction spending often doesn't serve students or taxpayers as well as it could, but it is important to establish up front that nearly all these less-than-optimal decisions are made by smart, caring, financially prudent people who do have student and taxpayer interests at heart. It is the system and the rules they operate within that creates the waste, not the people themselves.

Building New Schools

The largest, albeit least frequent, capital purchase is building a new school. No district can build a new school without consent of the voters. There is usually a special election or specific ballot question authorizing the funding and construction. This seems like a strong system of checks and balances, but it hasn't stopped many a new school from being built (or fully renovated from stump up) that probably needn't have been. There are a number of reasons for this.

A common reason for building a new school is because the old school wasn't well maintained. It is embarrassing for a guy who designed and built machinery to admit, but I don't take good care of my cars. Once, I went a long time without changing the oil—a very long time. I was busy, and everything seemed to be running fine, until the engine seized and the car wouldn't run. The cost of fixing the car exceeded its value, so it was logical that I buy a new car.

Many a school board and community find themselves in a similar situation. They have a rundown school that is too expensive to fix, so they build a new one. While this was prudent at the time, they too failed to maintain the facility, thus creating the need for a new building.

In my experience, spending money on building maintenance is not very popular with school boards, especially during tight budgets. When districts focus on "protecting the classroom"—an oft-heard cry during the budget season—they mean the people in the classroom, not the classroom itself. For several years, I watched a district put into its preliminary budget the money to repair a leaking roof, only to have the funds cut back by the school board in the final budget, providing only enough money to cover a few patches and lots of trash cans to catch the rain. On a bad day, you would see dozens of buckets catching water in the hallways. In time, the water weakened the ceiling and caused mold to form on the walls. There was no choice but to build a new school.

Building maintenance is not very sexy; it doesn't raise test scores, it doesn't raise teacher compensation; and it doesn't keep class size down.

It shifts resources from all the noble efforts, but in the long run building maintenance is a good investment and will actually free up funds for teaching and learning by extending the life of schools.

Given the political pressures, it is best if a school board or town establishes a fixed amount to be set aside or spent on building maintenance each year. *How* the money is spent should be debated, but not *if* the money will be spent.

A crumbling building isn't the only reason that new schools get built when it might not be required. A community's sense of neighborhood and fairness also drives a great deal of construction. "Fairness" has many definitions. As highlighted in chapter 4, some districts believe that one social worker per school is a fair allocation, even if some schools have two hundred students and others have two thousand. Another definition might demand that the staffing be proportional to enrollment or need. This "one per" mindset can carry over to big-ticket spending like new schools as well.

I have heard many a superintendent share thinking along these lines of "We have seen a lot of growth in the southern part of the district, so we will be building a few new schools in that region. The west also has two high schools that are falling down, which are included in the construction bond." So far, so good. At this point, the plan is needs based. The conversation continues, "Of course, we will have to renovate some buildings in the north and east as well." I assumed that the construction in the north and east was to broaden the base of support by giving each region something to vote for. "Yes, but" has been a common response. "Yes, but we need to have something for everyone; it wouldn't be fair to upgrade schools for some neighborhoods but not others."

The extra construction wasn't added because it's unfair to some *students*, but because it's unfair to some *neighborhoods*. Communities often have very close associations with their local elementary and high schools. A district not spreading the new construction around can feel insulting to one part of town or another. This feeling of local pride runs so strong that it can lead to building and keeping many more schools than needed. Virtually every superintendent of an urban district with a declining population has wrestled with the unwinnable dilemma of having too many schools.

Close Excess Schools: It's Hard, but Not Impossible

Districts that experience white flight or shifting enrollments find themselves with a lot more schools than children. Detroit, for example, saw enrollment drop by more than one hundred thousand students but closed few schools, resulting in at least sixty extra buildings. Similar stories can be told in many other northeastern and midwestern cities. As the charter movement has taken hold, the exodus has accelerated in some cities. In one urban district, for example, enrollment has declined steadily as more than five thousand students switched to charter schools from traditional public schools (and out of school buildings) over the last few years. Recent legislation will move another five thousand kids into charter schools over the next few years. Regardless of the reason, many urban districts have more schools than they need. This means more busing costs, more staffing costs, more maintenance and custodial costs, and a lot more of the hard-to-find annual facilities maintenance dollars.

If you are thinking, *why don't they just close the unneeded schools?* I suspect you have never been a superintendent or school board member. The public outcry—rage, actually—that accompanies such a decision can't be underestimated. In Oakland, California, a district wracked by budget cuts and dropping enrollment, recently proposed closing just five of its one hundred schools. As the local paper reported, "The contentious meeting was held in Oakland Technical High School's large auditorium, and the extra space was needed. Hundreds of teachers, families and other supporters arrived at the meeting en masse, after marching together up Broadway from Mosswood Park. Even before the meeting started, they began chanting: 'Save our schools!' . . . Many urged the board to reject the plan, arguing that the closure of historic neighborhood schools and the displacement of 1,000 students and staff members was not worth the $2 million annual savings the superintendent has projected."[1]

Nearly all the hue and cry is about damage to the neighborhood, deep personal insult, and sincere sense of loss. What might look like a falling-down, low-performing school is also the hub of a neighborhood's identity and self-worth.

There are a few ways to better navigate the minefield of excess capacity, but none are for the faint of heart.

Be Transparent About the Decision-Making Process

Which schools to close is never a simple choice. Trade-offs abound, such as:

- Close the schools in the worst physical condition. But what if one is a very high-performing school?
- Close the schools with the smallest enrollment to impact the fewest children. But what if one was recently renovated?
- Close the school with the worst academic performance. But what if one recently got a new principal, had half the staff replaced, and received millions of dollars of grant money?
- Close the schools with the biggest declines in enrollment and the most empty seats. But what if this impacts one racial minority group disproportionately?

The list could go on for pages, and none of these what-ifs are uncommon. Strangely enough, the worst thing the district leadership can do is try to wrestle in detail with all the complexities. That's right—in this scenario, detailed, case-by-case reasoned judgment can lead to disaster. One district with significant overcapacity wrestled for years trying to balance all the pros and cons, and in the end made a very thoughtful, but modest, recommendation to close a few schools. The outcry first came from the usual places, but it quickly spread. There seemed to be no logic to the choices, opponents argued. This was not at all true, but there was no *simple or clear* logic; the decision was a nuanced balancing of many conflicting factors, which can look inconsistent and arbitrary to the public. The parents hadn't spent years wrestling with the trade-offs. The subtleties are hard to explain in a sound bite. Why did you close the Kennedy School, when the Johnson School is older (or more rundown, or has lower test scores, or has fewer students, etc.)? This put the district on the defensive, and few supported its choices.

Learning from the experience, the district leadership went back to the drawing board and focused first on developing consensus on transparent criteria. Only after there was agreement on the relative priorities could the community understand the decision. Remember, since the closing of a school is a personal loss, it is important that the community feels the guidelines were objective. This moves the decision away from "You like them more than you like us."

Share the Decision-Making Responsibility Widely

"Uneasy lies the head that wears the crown," according to Shakespeare. I have met many superintendents who feel that the difficult decision to close a school is the work (hard and often unappreciated) of the senior leadership team, or worse yet, work for consultants. Few superintendents have the political capital to take all the heat and still survive as an empowered leader. It is human nature to shoot the messenger and hang the decision maker. If the process of deciding which schools to close is expanded to include principals and many central office staff members, then the superintendent gains both their buy-in and political capital.

The first step for this large decision-making group is, paradoxically, a step backward. Explain in detail why schools must be closed. Give the decision-making team time and information to push back on the very idea of closing schools. Entertain and investigate all the alternatives that will, undoubtedly, be suggested by the public (e.g., couldn't we cut out summer professional development; couldn't we cut back the gifted and talented program?). Rather than quickly dismissing these ideas, investigate and quantify the savings. In a short time, the community and the large decision-making team will learn, and more importantly, believe, that nothing else saves similar dollars as closing unneeded capacity.

One district that used this process was able to convince more than sixty principals and other leaders that unless they reduced the number of empty seats by closing some schools, they would be reducing hundreds of classroom teachers instead.

Once the large decision-making group has accepted that schools must close, collectively set the criteria. Don't jump to the list of schools, but focus instead on the guidelines. In less than an hour, the team members will realize that this is a hard, nuanced process with no obvious right answer. If they engage in setting the criteria, however, they will be better able to support the final outcome.

The support of principals is critical. Technically, the school board decides whether and which schools get closed. Often, however, it is the court of public opinion that decides. The public seems to trust principals and teachers more than superintendents and school boards. Thousands of private conversations, not the televised school board debates, can determine the outcome. When a teacher says in a faculty meeting, "Can you believe they are closing Kennedy School?!" a principal who participated in the entire process is likely to chime in, "It's a hard decision; there were no good choices, but if we don't close it, we will lay off two hundred more teachers, probably some in our school." Had the principal been excluded from the decision-making process, she might have otherwise nodded in agreement and suggested cutting summer professional development instead.

Often, parents—especially those with deep ties to the community and lots of private communication channels—will seek out the principal or lower-level central office staff to get the inside scoop. Again, involvement and understanding is the only way to get "good press" in these influential private conversations.

Rally Supporters, Rather Than Appease the Injured, by Stressing the Gains

School closings mean lots of meetings with angry parents and staff. Unfortunately, nothing said will likely make them happy. Certainly, there is nothing the district leadership could say that would please me if my neighborhood school were closing. Those impacted will still crowd the school board meeting and say the superintendent doesn't love children.

Sometimes districts forget to rally the people who will benefit from the closures—all the other parents. Schools are closed so that money can be shifted to support children's learning. One district, facing a monstrous budget gap, made the case that closing ten schools would save $20 million a year, which in turn would save 250 classroom teachers, which in turn would keep down class sizes. All of a sudden, closing ten schools meant smaller classes in the other hundred-plus schools. This helped galvanize support from teachers, principals, and parents in the schools that were staying open.

Consider if Charter Schools Are the Problem or the Answer

Some people love charter schools, and others hate them. Regardless of where you stand, charter schools do exist, and for each student who attends one, there is an empty seat left behind in the traditional public schools.

In most cities, charter school leaders bemoan their substandard space, hope to raise a capital fund to buy or build a facility, and complain that they are at a financial disadvantage due to higher occupancy costs. The lack of high-quality facilities hasn't seemed to stem the tide of parents opting for charter schools. In nearly every city, there is a waiting list for charter schools, despite often-subpar space. In short, in many cities, traditional public schools have too many buildings, and charter schools have too few. This is the making of a win-win deal. Remember, denying charter schools quality buildings doesn't slow the exodus, but it does place a lot of "our" students in rundown or ill-suited school houses.

Renting or selling excess buildings to charters will reduce costs and increase revenue. Renting *part* of a school may solve even more problems. Since closing a school tends to bring out a mob, a district can keep the peace and still get much of the same savings by keeping all of its schools open, but renting some floors or wings to charter schools. I visited one such split school in Brooklyn, New York. Other than two signs

A CRAZY IDEA?

Learn from Congress?

Taken together, these four steps can help districts better manage excess capacity. There might be a fifth strategy, but I have never seen it tried in the K–12 world. It's an idea that comes from the US Congress. It does seem odd to look to Congress for advice on how to make tough decisions, but consider this example. When Congress tried to confront excess military bases, every attempt failed as the impacted constituents lobbied for saving their bases and closing others instead. This is the same problem school boards face. After many failed efforts to reduce excess capacity (and the associated costs), Congress created the Base Realignment and Closure (BRAC) commission. Essentially, a small group of people weighed all the nuances and needs and created the cut list. Congress could accept or reject the list, but not change it. This empowered it to vote for the cuts, while criticizing the list at the same time. "I would save your base, (or school), but my hands are tied."

out front, nothing else changed, except that the kids on the second floor all wore uniforms. The charter school operated on the second floor and didn't disturb life on the first floor.

Build New Schools More Cost-Effectively

As populations shift and grow, some districts will need to build new schools. Accepting that nearly all municipal construction costs more than similar private-sector projects, we still have a number of possible options to reduce the spread but get a great, well-built school house.

The roles and guidelines for new school construction vary by state, so not all the issues and options apply universally. Much of the added costs stem from the design, or more specifically, the design process. A detailed study by the Massachusetts School Building Authority found that, on average, elementary and middle schools were built about 32 percent bigger than state DOE guidelines, and high schools were a full 39 percent oversized.[2]

In Massachusetts, for example, a district planning to build a school starts by hiring an architect. Seems logical, but is it? Has any other district in the country built an elementary school for three hundred students before? Obviously, it has. Why not use (or start with) well-tested, existing blueprints? Companies that build shopping malls, condo complexes, and homes often use predesigned plans as the basis for the next project. Yes, they learn and improve from prior projects, but they don't start from scratch. Some will argue that every community is different, but are they all completely unique? One town that built two similarly sized elementary schools just a few years apart started both projects' designs from scratch. Each project budgeted about $1.5 million for design fees. The second school saved nothing in design cost from the prior project.

When the private sector does design from scratch, most large construction projects turn to "design-build" firms. This is a combination architecture and construction firm, and it can bring about big savings. Architects, on the whole, focus much more on functionality and aesthetics, but not ease of construction. They design and then contractors bid on providing the school exactly as rendered. It turns out, for example, that one- and three-story schools are much more cost-effective than two-story schools. Given the space and expense of stairwells and elevators, once you add these extras, there isn't much additional cost to going up a floor, and the total footprint is reduced. If an architect designs a two-story school, the low bidder is the company that can build the lowest-cost two-story school, and the three-story option can't be considered. Design-build firms compete on total project cost, and have the in-house expertise to make cost-design trade-offs.

Let's take a step back. How are the architects chosen in the first place? In many suburban districts, it starts with the building committee—a group of volunteers appointed to oversee a large-scale construction project. It is not uncommon for half the committee to comprise a few small-time contractors (think deck and kitchen builders) and a few independent general contractors who build houses in the community, and the other half to comprise concerned citizens or town officials who have never been involved in any construction, save their own homes' deck or kitchen renovations. Often, the school administrators aren't even voting members of the committee. Despite their best intentions, the design and oversight of a $20 million elementary school or $150 million high school is left to people who are not experts in construction or education. They rely on the architect for a great deal of guidance; they also often select the architect.

In the new school construction projects I have followed, the fees the architects charge were fixed as a percentage of project cost. This means they don't compete on price, so their sales pitches stress two points: first, that they have designed a lot of schools before (many of them *only* design schools), and second, that they will listen to the building committee and the community. It seemed to me that the more they promised *not* to lead but to follow, the higher they were rated by the committee and thus the more likely they were to be hired. This created a role reversal.

This "we will give you what you want" architect approach goes into hyperdrive during the needs assessment (aka wish list) phase of the work. The winning architect conducts a long series of interviews with every possible stakeholder group. The science department head "needs" dedicated science rooms, each with lab tables; the music department "needs" practice rooms, an auditorium, and soundproof classrooms; and on it goes. This is how the average school in Massachusetts came to be a third bigger (and thus a third more expensive) than state DOE guidelines recommend.

There are a number of problems with this approach. There is no pressure to make trade-offs, or to balance cost versus benefit. There is also no system to think about double-dipping—using one space for multiple purposes. Should the library also be designed for small instruction when library isn't in session? Should occupational therapy rooms also function as music practice rooms? They are about the same size, often empty, and soundproof (or at least, out of the way).

One of the biggest differences between private-sector and school design is exemplified by how much multipurpose space is designed into a new office building, for example, compared to a school. The biggest difference, however, is the planner's time frame. Many private-sector buildings assume space use will change over time. They are designed so that office space can be switched to conference space, or so the engineering department can expand or contract over time and the space will still accommodate its unique needs.

School design tends to focus tightly on current needs and instructional models, even though the building has a fifty-year-plus useful life. For example, a school is often designed with the exact number of kindergarten classes that the ten-year forecast suggests. If fewer are actually needed, these rooms—with their bathrooms and low counters and interior half-walls—won't serve as a first-grade room. In one elementary school construction project, science was, at the time, being taught by a specialized teacher, so the school built a science room with huge, immovable lab desks. In short order, that instructional model was abandoned, and the room was subsequently only good for staff birthday parties. Often, woodshop, computer labs, art rooms, language labs, and libraries are built for one use and only one use. Lastly, the space is designed for the current program offerings. The school housing the preschool or autism class gets a special room just for that need. Does anyone expect that the programs won't move or close over the next fifty years?

After each department develops its wish list and rough layouts are drafted, the committee does start the process of balancing competing needs and making trade-offs. But this process also differs from the private sector. In many business settings, the discussions center on value—"Is it worth it?" Yes, a conference room in each wing would be nice, but it takes up too much space that will be empty most of the day. The same discussion for a school tends to center on, "Do we have the budget?" Many school projects start with the final price in hand. A bond is passed to build a $50 million school, so the goal is to spend all $50 million. Spending $45 million feels like we are denying kids lots of stuff, rather than saving money. A vicious cycle ensues because each community sets its budget based on recently built schools, where they spent the maximum of their budgets.

The deliberations of a building committee in one fiscally conservative town exemplify this challenge. The basketball coach wanted an extra court so that the J.V. team could practice during a varsity game. Due to space limitations, the court would be next to wetlands, requiring very expensive construction. The incremental cost for the court was $3 million. To put this in perspective, the very same district had questioned the value of paying a few thousand dollars a year for the freshman and J.V. coaching stipends, but was seriously considering a multimillion-dollar practice court that would be needed for only a few hours a week, a few months a year. Sure, the space would be used year-round, but it was only suggested (wished for) because of an infrequent scheduling conflict. I assumed the eye-popping cost would kill the idea. Two weeks later, the architects announced with great excitement that the practice court fit in the budget! Rather than concluding that the budget was too high, the building committee approved the court. For people that waited for sales and drove a bit farther to save a few cents on gas, this seemed quite an unlikely decision!

In my follow-up conversations with committee members, they shared that they felt the court was, in fact, on sale. The state, they pointed out, paid more than half the cost of new school construction, so instead of spending $3 million, they were saving $1.5 million! And, of course, they reminded me that it was in the budget.

The last and maybe most insidious list generated during the design process is the *alternate list*. This is a formal, spend-every-dollar wish list. If, by chance, the final project comes in under budget, extra items will be purchased, such as more smartboards, more athletic equipment, or the like.

Quality and efficiency guru Edward Deming said, "Every system is perfectly designed for the result it gets." The school construction system is designed to spend the budget and fulfill the wish lists, rather than build a flexible, high-quality building at the lowest reasonable cost.

From the taxpayer's perspective, a dollar is a dollar, but often I have seen how some expenses just feel better than others. Health insurance, central office staff, and superintendent raises are not fun expenditures, but facilities are. Many people feel good about spending money on school buildings. One district, for example, voted to expand the library—including state-of-the-art technology, small-group reading rooms, and conference space—as part of a school expansion. A few weeks later, essentially the same group cut librarians and all books for the new library. This irony was explained as follows: "The expanded library is forever, and the other expenditures are in the operating budget." While often viewed as separate, every extra dollar spent on new construction is one less dollar over time that taxpayers have to support the operating budget.

Invest in Construction Oversight and Project Financial Management

Once the school is designed and construction starts, there are a few expenses worth spending on, yet this is when some building committees insist on frugality. Construction oversight and project financial management are great investments.

Building a new school takes a year or two, and a lot can go wrong. In theory, the architect monitors the contractor, and the contractor is responsible for meeting the specs on time and on budget. The challenge is that the architect tends to want to preserve the design, while the contractor tends to be more practical. Who mediates the conflict? Sometimes it's the building committee, the principal, or the superintendent. None has the experience to make an informed judgment. An experienced construction project manager who works for the district, not the architect or the construction company, is worth his weight in gold.

The other staff position worth hiring is a project finance manager. The number of bills, change orders, and documents required for state reimbursement is mind-numbing. It can be a costly mistake to put this added responsibility on the district CFO. One small district opted to save $85,000 and tasked the district staff to manage the construction budget for its new school. The staff had no experience with expenditures crossing school years, had difficulty tracking partial payments, and unknowingly overspent by millions. Once the error was discovered, truckloads of supplies, furniture, and technology were returned unopened to cover the deficit.

While it might not be obvious that a school CFO isn't a skilled construction finance manager, it should be more obvious that a school principal isn't trained to be a general contractor. In the case of adding a wing or rebuilding an existing school, the principal often becomes the project manager. I have chatted with principals who confessed that they hadn't observed teachers in the last few months or looked at student data from the current year, but who could tell me that the blue tile for the first-floor bathroom was due in on Tuesday, the drop ceilings in rooms 101, 102, and 103 had been fixed, and the painters were expected to start in ten days. One of the hidden costs of a school renovation is that the principal might stop being an instructional leader and instead become the construction site foreman.

The school construction process in many districts is overly costly, but some districts and states have addressed the shortcomings. Collectively, these lessons learned are summed up in "Ten Best Practices for School Construction Projects."

Save Big with Smaller Capital Projects

Most districts won't be building a new school next year or in the near future, but many have buildings that need minor renovations or repairs. Like their big brother, new construction, these smaller capital projects can also be much more cost-effective. Once again, the culprit is the system. I have seen time and time again the opportunity to reduce project costs by 75 percent or more without sacrificing quality. In most cases, it has been an uphill battle to spend less, because the lower-cost solution bucks the system.

The crux of this battle is often that decision makers understand the problem, not the solution, and they in turn rely on experts who under-

---

Ten Best Practices for School Construction Projects

1. Design a school on the assumption that rooms and spaces will be used for different purposes in the future, some of which may not even exist yet. Who could have forecasted the need for online learning, biotech, or nanotechnology classes twenty years ago?
2. Design spaces to serve multiple purposes during the course of a school week.
3. Consider design-build firms or architects that have experience in the private sector as well as in public schools.
4. Fill building oversight committees with seasoned professionals experienced in large-scale construction.
5. Hire an independent project manager and project finance manager.
6. Create an incentive such that unspent funds will be used for future projects.
7. Create a culture that rewards coming in under budget. This could include gain sharing the savings with the architect and/or general contractor.
8. Keep the principal in the classroom, not on the worksite.
9. Remember that what happens in the classroom matters more than the physical classroom, and that every dollar spent on construction is one less dollar for instruction.
10. Never forget that $1 million is still a lot of money, even if it is in the budget or subsidized by the state.

---

stand the solution, but not the problem. A quick example from my time as superintendent can help make this point.

Problem: Our servers (the computers that comprise the district's network) are overheating.

Solution: Air-condition the server room at a cost of $75,000. Failure to do so could destroy the servers, and worse yet, wipe out the student data, e-mail system, and special education records.

A better solution: Spend $10,000 to air-condition the server room.

The best solution: Spend $1,000 and move the servers to a room that is already air-conditioned.

Here's the irony; the $75,000 solution was everyone's first choice, and the less expensive options caused a stir. The story unfolded as follows. The servers overheated one summer day. Fortunately, the data was backed up, but this was a wake-up call. The head of technology rightfully viewed this as a real problem. Not knowing much, nothing actually, about cooling servers, he reached out to an expert. He had two choices: hire an engineer to "spec" the solution, or get a vendor to do some research for free. Vendors are often very happy to provide advice at no charge so that they can help shape the solution to their strengths and increase their odds of winning the soon-to-be-issued public bid. In this case, the vendor recommended an X YZ super-duper air conditioner. All told, it would cost about $75,000. Sample specifications were provided.

The IT head asked permission to put the project out to bid. To ensure that the district spends money wisely, state law requires posting the specification and request for proposal (RFP) in the local papers and on the Web, and to circulate it widely. Each vendor would receive detailed requirements of what we wanted to purchase. The lowest bid would win, ensuring that tax dollars were spent wisely. I said no!

"So you don't care if the servers crash?" I was asked. I cared a lot, but couldn't get my head around $75,000 for air-conditioning one room. My IT director insisted I meet with the vendor who spec'd the job. The vendor explained that there was no other way to meet our needs; anything else would not do what we wanted. This was an interesting statement. What exactly did we want, and who decided? "What problem are we solving?" I asked. Flipping through his notes, the vendor rattled off: "Cool fifty thousand BTUs today in an eight-hundred-square-foot room, plus 50 percent more in the future."

Now the questions started flying. How did we know we needed to cool fifty thousand BTUs today? We didn't. No one could find the heat specs on our servers, so we guessed high to play it safe. Who determined we wanted to cool 50 percent more in the future? The IT director had mentioned we could be adding more servers in the future, and 50 percent seemed like a safe guess. And lastly, why did he care how big the room was? "Volume is everything!" the vendor shouted. "We have to move the air; twice as much air means twice as much cooling."

I kicked the project back to the drawing board. After Googling the make and model of each server, we found the current heat draw was only twenty thousand BTUs, not fifty thousand. More surprisingly to us (an air-conditioning salesman, the IT director, and a superintendent, all of whom knew, and should know, little about servers), new servers generate much *less* heat, and our future requirements would drop, not increase. These facts alone dropped the cost to $35,000. I still wasn't happy, so I set up one more meeting. I kept asking for options to get the price down, and everyone was content that we had already "saved" $40,000, but I still saw it as spending $35,000.

I'm embarrassed to say, all these meetings and debates took place in my office. In an act of frustration, I said, "Let's move this conversation to the server room to see if that jogs any ideas." A bit bewildered, we took a left at the end of a hallway instead of a right and went to the *new* server room. I didn't know we had a new server room, but I didn't need to know. When I walked into the room, everything immediately became clear. The servers didn't fill the room; in fact, they were smaller than a kitchen fridge, sitting in an extra-large classroom. We were trying to cool ten times more space than was needed. "What if we built a closet-sized room in the corner to house the servers?" I asked. The response: "Oh, then you could use a simple unit for about $5,000!" Frustrated, I asked why we wouldn't just build a few walls for a few thousand dollars. "Maintenance said they are too busy, and the AC vendor doesn't do construction," said the IT director.

There are a lot of lessons to be learned from this sad story. Keep in mind, the IT director was smart, caring, never wasteful, and always tried to put the needs of the district first. This was not his fault. It was my fault (and the system's).

My first lesson was to not assume a department head is the most qualified to manage a capital equipment project. In the same year, my foreign language head was expected to outfit a language lab, and my drama teacher to spec the renovation of our stage lights and curtains. Both encountered similar issues.

The second lesson was to be explicit and thoughtful in naming the problem. We had asked to cool the whole room when we should have asked how to keep the servers from overheating without spending much money. It may seem obvious to carefully describe the problem, but it's tricky. A few years later, we wanted to fix or replace all the exterior doors in one school. This was a long-overdue project, and some grant funds had become available. History repeated itself when the contractor, who was helping spec the work, mentioned in passing, "I'm sure you want new jambs too, right?" The principal, who was tasked with getting the estimate, said, "Sure." Here is the rub: the jamb is the frame of the door, and most of them were embedded in concrete walls. Replacing the jambs, which weren't in bad shape, tripled the cost of the project.

The third lesson is that it is a terrible use of a superintendent's time to micromanage small construction projects. Since I had a background in manufacturing, factory construction, and engineering, I knew enough to know we weren't getting good value for our construction dollars. But it was still a bad use of my time.

The fourth and most important lesson is that school districts need to have industrial engineers on their staff, or to hire them as needed. An industrial engineer is a jack of all trades who bounces from project to project doing research, checking out alternative solutions, conducting cost-benefit analysis, and homing in on the question, "What problem do we really need to solve?" In the case of the servers overheating, the real problem was that the librarian had kicked someone out of her office, who in turn moved into the server room, and who subsequently didn't like the servers crowding her new workspace; so, we had moved the servers into an empty room, which wasn't air-conditioned.

If you think your district has an industrial engineer on staff, you are probably mistaken, unless it is a very large district. Most districts do have a head of maintenance, who is practical and also a jack of all trades, but that person has more often than not come up through the ranks and learned how to fix broken things along the way. This is not the same as an engineer, who typically has a master's degree and a penchant for systems thinking.

Try Solution-Based Contracting

Lots of districts do seek outside help with overseeing repair and renovation projects rather than saddle the school or district staff—but this is no assurance that the outcome will be any better. Districts often look to architects or design engineers to write the specifications for a public bid. The underlying assumption is that if lots of people bid on the project, the district will get the best price. It may get the best price on the wrong solution, however.

One of my schools had a courtyard that leaked water, lots of water, into a locker room beneath it. Using a typical public-sector process, the district hired an architect to help. He worked up detailed specifications: where to replace the cement, what type of flashing to use, where each drainage trough should start and stop, etc. The anticipated cost was $400,000 to $600,000. After the bids were received, we would know the true price and hire the lowest bidder. Fear of contractors cutting corners leads to very detailed specs, costing the district $30,000 or more in this case just to get ready for the bid. Strangely, if the contractor didn't stop the leaking but did follow the specifications, no one would be at fault, but we still wouldn't be able to use the locker room.

This process is widely used in municipal purchasing, but it's not nearly as common in the private sector. Many private companies take a different approach. They describe the problem, such as "Water is leaking in. We don't want this; please stop it." No more detail, no hundreds of pages of specs. Companies will typically also add, "You have to guarantee that the water won't come in, or you will redo it until it's right." The next step in the private-sector process is for lots of contractors to look at the problem, think about it, and then propose both a solution and accompanying price. This generates lots of alternative approaches.

We tried something similar with the leaky courtyard, and one novel solution surfaced: "If no one used the courtyard, we can place a rubber membrane (like a roof) and seal it up tight for $80,000." It turns out, the courtyard was off-limits to students and was only used a few days in the spring by a handful of teachers eating their lunch. The bid spec process would never have yielded this outcome. In fact, it would have disqualified the bidder altogether.

This isn't a radical idea, since school districts regularly ask for more solution-based proposals for services, but it is much less common in school construction and maintenance.

Keep Instructional Materials out of the Closet

There is one more type of capital purchase worth thinking differently about, but it doesn't always seem like "capital equipment." Since textbooks, instructional software, and computer hardware last for more than three years, they, too, are capital purchases. They are also an area of potential savings. The question of *which* instructional materials are worth purchasing is discussed in chapters 5 and 7. *How* to buy them is the topic at hand.

How much a district spends on any given textbook adoption is a simple calculation: the cost for one multiplied by the quantity. Both sides of this equation can sometimes be improved. Let's start with the unit cost. At first glance, it should be easy to know if a district is getting a good price on a textbook, but it's not. In fact, the whole selling process seems designed to make it hard. For the sake of example, let's follow the purchase of a new elementary math textbook for a district with ten thousand students.

The textbook is $100 per book, the classroom kit is $495 per classroom, the teacher's guide is $200 per teacher, and the training is extra. If you buy everything, then the vendor will give a discount and throw in the training for free. This may sound like a good deal to the math department head, who is the point person on this purchase. Saving over $30,000 on $300,000 seems like a good deal. Table 8.1 does the simple math to calculate the total cost of $300,000.

In my experience, many schools would place the order at this point. Some don't even get the 10 percent discount. When I asked, "Why no discount on such a big order?" one department head responded with a huff, "I'm not at a flea market, haggling. These are quality materials. That's what they cost, and it's unprofessional to bicker over price." What she really meant to say was, "I hate to negotiate, and the salesperson is lovely and has offered free training, which I feel guilty about in the first place. I'm worried she won't get paid for her time, which isn't fair."

Create a Buying Team

Too often, the person best qualified to select the curriculum materials may not be the best person to handle the negotiations. Many districts realize this and try to address the concern through competitive bidding or by having the business office handle the transaction. Unfortunately,

Table 8.1

Textbook purchasing—typical example

Item	Quantity	Unit cost	Total cost
Textbook	2,500	$100	$250,000
Teacher's guide	120	$200	$24,000
Classroom kit	120	$495	$59,400
Training	3 days	Free	$0
Shipping	1 shipment	Didn't ask	?
Subtotal			$333,400
Discount			($33,340)
Total			$300,060
Shipping			$33,340
Real total			**$333,400**

these options don't work well for curriculum material because there is only one vendor who provides the desired material. No one does, or should, select a math program because publisher A bid less than publisher B. The decision to go with publisher A was already made, so the competitive bid process won't yield true competition. Also, the business office, which might be better at hard bargaining, may not actually have a tough negotiator on staff. Often, the purchasing function is more focused on compliance (did we follow procedures?) than haggling well. Finally, the business office can't decide whether the classroom kits are needed or if 100, rather than 125, teacher guides are required.

So what's the big deal with the scenario depicted in table 8.1? The district got the textbooks it wanted, and saved 10 percent. The problem is, it could have purchased the math program at half the cost! Worst of all, it didn't even get 10 percent off in the end. The publisher charges a flat 10 percent for shipping, which it forgot to mention.

I learned what is possible when buying curriculum materials only through luck. As superintendent, I led an effort to vertically align our K–12 curriculum, which meant we would be buying a lot of textbooks and such. The knowledge of which materials would meet our needs rested in the brains of my department heads. They each spent months researching options and made thoughtful choices. For a purchase this size, I typically held a final review meeting before approving it.

My science department head opened the meeting by handing out a typed purchase order and asking for permission to spend the remaining 50 percent of her budget on other projects. I was annoyed, and I made it clear that the money was specifically earmarked for vertical alignment purchases, and the idea of buying only half the materials in an effort to get funds for other pet projects was unacceptable. She shot back, "We are getting 100 percent of the textbooks, materials, and supplies, but at half the price!" Now I was intrigued. After a mumbled apology, I asked how. "I like to haggle," she responded. "After eight rounds of negotiations and two threats to take our business elsewhere, they agreed to 30 percent off list price. Then I went to work on shipping costs. They charge 10 percent, but I arranged the shipping directly with UPS and saved another 6 percent. I only had to ask, and they threw in free training. Also, when I looked closely at all the materials, I realized some weren't aligned with our state curriculum, so we cut them from the order. Finally, I looked inside the kits and realized a bunch of the stuff could be bought from Staples for a lot less." In short, she bargained hard and shopped wisely.

Excited by the deal and frustrated by the fact that other subjects didn't get such a bargain, I asked the science head to help negotiate the other departments' curriculum materials. This was radical and resented by all. Cries of "It's not her department," "It's insulting," and "She won't know what to buy!" filled the room. After much cajoling and smoothing of bruised egos, they set off to jointly purchase the materials.

So what can a few hours of hard bargaining and thoughtful purchasing do to a $300,000 purchase of math materials? Turns out, this hypothetical but all too typical district was buying textbooks for grades K–5, but kindergarten didn't plan to use them.

The district was buying them "just in case they change their minds, and to be complete." The teacher's guides, upon inspection, were not very helpful. The district opted to buy only one per grade in each building. The classroom kits were an outrage, containing mostly overpriced file folders, blank labels, pencils, and a few posters. The team arranged the shipping themselves and of course got a 25 percent discount on the books through tough negotiations. As frosting on the cake, they found 250 copies of the textbook at an online used-book store in mint condition—one year old and 50 percent off. At the end of the day, the district could get everything it needed at 50 percent less, as table 8.2 illustrates.

Some readers may be wondering if the scenario in table 8.1 is just an isolated example of a clueless department head being taken advantage of, but in my travels, I hear similar stories—including millions of dollars of instructional software licenses never being used, and textbooks still in their packaging five years after being purchased. I seldom hear of 30 percent discounts, however. As outlined in "Checklist for Buying New Textbooks and Curriculum Materials," there are some simple questions you can consider before buying instructional materials to help you make better-informed and cost-effective decisions.

The root cause of overspending is that the knowledge of what to buy and the skills to bargain hard and purchase wisely are different, but districts don't often create a buying team with both skill sets. When most people walk into a store, they hope to get what they need at a good price. Sure, that end-of-the-aisle display may persuade us to buy two extra-large bags of Fritos that we didn't really need, or a good salesman

Table 8.2

Textbook purchasing—hard bargaining and careful planning

Item	Quantity	Unit cost	Total cost
Textbook, new	1,750	$100	$175,000
Textbook, used	250	$50	$12,500
Teacher's guide	40	$200	$8,000
Classroom kit	100	$200	$20,000
Training	3 days	Free	$0
Shipping	1 shipment		$10,000
Subtotal			$225,500
Discount			($53,250)
Total			**$172,250**

Checklist for Buying New Textbooks and Curriculum Materials

___ Does the material fill an identified need based on student achievement data?

___ Have teachers and principals expressed a high level of dissatisfaction with the existing materials?

___ Are the quantities based on the minimum needed for year 1 implementation?

___ Are the materials available used?

___ Are the materials available new or like new on sites like eBay?

___ Can teacher guides be shared?

___ Can the related supplies be purchased from an office supply store?

___ Can UPS ship the materials for less than the vendor?

___ Is free training included?

___ Have three rounds of hard bargaining taken place?

---

will convince us that eighty more watts and four more speakers are worth the $1,000 for an upgraded radio in a new car, but we still try to spend no more than we have to and look for value. Many of these cost- and value-conscious shoppers turn into something quite different when purchasing for a public school. Often, they spend as much as they can, and common sense can give way to defensive buying.

Nearly every salesperson dealing with schools knows that after "Hello, how are you?" the first question is, "What's your budget?" Many capital projects are included as line items in either the operating, capital, or grant budget. Districts guess months in advance what the new boiler or textbook adoption will cost. This is intended to be the maximum approved expenditure. For many reasons, it also becomes the minimum. If a district has $300,000 allotted for textbooks and the quote is $300,000, it is likely to just buy them, rather than haggle. Sure, if the quote were $350,000, it would haggle down to $300,000 (but often not $275,000). Worse, if the program costs $280,000, many buyers will typically add $20,000 worth of extras to top off the order to spend the whole budget.

I don't want to be too critical because I have done all of this, many times. Crazy as it seems, given the rules in my district, it made some sense. Budget line items were often "use it or lose it." If I didn't spend the full amount, the money would disappear. There was no incentive to spend less. The same is true of construction projects, whether it's a new heating system or a new school.

Beyond just spending all the money we have in our pocket, K–12 purchasing is much more risk-averse than spending in our private lives. There can be so much pressure to not waste the taxpayers' money that districts spend forty times more than needed just to be sure they won't. I have noticed that school districts ask for engineers (at $150–$250 an hour) to help with the smallest capital purchases, when other industries or individuals wouldn't. My favorite—actually, least favorite—example comes from my days as a school board member. The problem was simple. For a few weeks in June, our computer lab got really hot. After eight years of staff complaints, the school board decided to act. We authorized purchasing two window air-conditioning units for the room, at a total cost of about $900. A month later, rather than learning that units were installed, the board was presented with a request for $3,500 for HVAC engineering for the computer lab.

The facilities director wasn't certain that two window units would do the trick. Despite my protests, the committee eventually decided it would undermine the community's confidence in our fiscal management if we paid for something that didn't work well. This fear translated to the consulting engineer, who reported back that the only way to be certain that we could fully cool the lab no matter what the outside temperature (up to a hundred degrees) was to install a rooftop unit, which of course required upgraded wiring in the room as well. Since we had no other air conditioning in the school and I actually expected the room would be hot on a hundred-degree day, I voted for the $900 window units. My colleagues, all fiscally conservative in their private lives, felt it only prudent to spend $30,000 on the rooftop unit to be certain.

Big one-time purchases—from high school textbooks to entire high schools—are large, complex financial transactions. By ensuring that people with the right skills and incentives are part of the buying process, districts will stretch limited dollars.

Better Information

FORGING THE PATH TO
BETTER DECISIONS

*Managing a budget is hard, but it's even harder when insightful
information is either unavailable or hidden. Creating detailed
budget documents and a team approach to building budgets will
yield smarter budgets.*

Ever drive to a new restaurant without knowing for sure where it is
located? You know it's downtown by the theater, which gets you in the
right neighborhood. After spending a lot of time driving around looking for it, you eventually arrive twenty minutes late with an apology.
I've done this many times. Would you ever drive to the same restaurant
blindfolded? Not likely, but as superintendent, I often felt like I was
driving with my eyes covered during the budget season. Sticking with
the metaphor, wouldn't it be nice to have GPS turn-by-turn instructions
for managing the district budget?

Management guru Peter Drucker said, "What gets measured gets
managed," and this is true of school budgets as well. Unfortunately,
many school districts don't measure the kinds of information needed to

tightly manage the district finances, and worse, the systems and culture are designed to hide, blur, and obscure the very information superintendents and school boards need most. Many of the ideas discussed in the prior chapters assume a great deal of information. Staffing to enrollment requires knowing exactly how many students will be in each class, how many kids want to take each course, how many hours a support teacher is working with students, how many English language learner (ELL) students are in each grade and building, and on the list goes. Using academic return on investment (A-ROI) requires measuring student gains and fully loaded program costs. Special education costs will never be fully managed without detailed knowledge of student needs and staff schedules. In most districts, little or none of this information is readily available. What I knew as a school board member and superintendent was that everyone was very busy and every program very effective. When nasty budget fights broke out, and none are meaner than budget debates, each party assumed different levels of program effectiveness to suit its case and bandied about half-truths as gospel.

I didn't want it to be this way. When I started as superintendent, I set out to get an overview of how the district spent its money. It was a simple request—I needed to know how many teachers the district had by type (grade or subject); how many custodians, administrators, etc.; plus other major nonpersonnel costs, such as utilities, maintenance, big contracts, and the like. My CFO, who was very smart, detail-oriented, and experienced, said if he made it a priority, I could get it in four weeks. The town had approved the budget a few months earlier, so I had assumed that getting this information required only the push of a button. Reluctantly, I waited the month, which stretched into six weeks.

The report I got wasn't worth the wait. Some lines were obviously wrong; for example, it excluded administrators I had met with just a day earlier. This prompted me to push for detailed backup data. I learned that the report overcounted custodians by 15 percent, undercounted special education teachers by 65 percent, and missed one-third of the administrators. I also learned that we spent $25.40 on occupational therapist travel and $1 million on special ed "other," which no one could define. With alarm, I also learned that we underestimated maintenance costs by half. Upset and worried, I quizzed my CFO. With some digging, he found answers to all of my questions. Custodians who resign are taken off the staff list, but not those out on sick or injury leave. This meant janitors who were gone for years, weren't being paid, and weren't coming back were still listed. The army of missing special education teachers was paid by federal grants, so the CFO didn't know who they were or how many we had. (He was the CFO, but this seemed like a reasonable response to him.) Most importantly, he assured me there was no need to worry about maintenance being underfunded, because "we overfund heating costs to cover both maintenance and textbooks."

If you're thinking what I was thinking, which was *this guy is in over his head*, you'd be as wrong as I was. We were a district with a reputation for strong financial management, the town won accolades for its sophisticated budgeting, and the CFO was definitely smarter than the average bear. The system was broken, not any one person. Of the fifty or so districts I have studied, about two-thirds are capable of creating no more detailed budget data than what I inherited, and only 10 percent can push a button and get the kind of detailed staffing and expense reports most similarly sized private-sector firms have at their fingertips.

One of the primary reasons that actual spending and staffing information is so elusive is that most school districts don't have one budget, but rather ten or fifty budgets. Each of these budgets has a different chart of accounts, uses different names for the same line item, and is developed and managed by different people; thus, the budgets can't be easily combined to paint a comprehensive picture.

The *operating budget* is the largest and most public budget, but it's not the only one. Each grant has its own separate budget, such as Title I, IDEA (Individuals with Disabilities Education Act; special education federal support), special education preschool federal support, and so on. A small district might have six or seven significant separate grant budgets, while a large urban district will have many dozens. Certain activities like food service will be set up as revolving accounts or enterprise funds that also have separate budgets. These are common when there is a separate revenue source, like lunch sales. Finally, there can be "off budget" expenses, such as health insurance, pension costs, bond debt, construction projects, crossing guards, or custodians, which can be on the town or city budget but charged back to the district.

This multitude of budgets isn't just a CPA's academic concern; it is a major obstacle to wisely managing a district's funds. In most districts, only the operating budget is subject to intense scrutiny. In a suburban district, the operating budget will often be no more than 85 to 90 percent of total spending, and can be as little as 75 percent. In urban districts, the operating budget can be as little as 65 percent or less of total spending. When I asked my CFO for a list of all employees, he gave me the partial response because, like most CFOs, he only managed the operating budget and thus only gave me the people paid through that source.

The bias to ignore all but the operating budget runs deep in many districts. In an informal poll of district CFOs asked, "What was the district's total spending last year?" over 90 percent reported just the operating budget expenses. They forgot to include all the other expenses. In another example, I was asked to help one district that was wrestling with a monstrous budget shortfall; more than 10 percent of total spending had to be cut. I was ushered into the war room, which had piles of papers spread out on a long table and flip charts with all the possible options. The district leaders had been meeting for two months and wanted my advice on how to quantify the impact of the proposed cuts. Despite the mountains of paper and the long list of ideas, they had considered only the operating budget. In the midst of the worst budget crisis in their history, federal grants, revolving funds, and off-budget expenses, all of which accounted for about 20 percent of total district spending, hadn't been reviewed or put on the table.

Returning to Drucker's "What gets measured gets managed," what does that mean for spending that is hardly visible, let alone measured? In low-spending, frugal districts, I have seen a great deal of excess in the less visible "other budgets." A few of the worst examples include:

- The part-time teacher earning $1,000 an hour
- New laptops unopened for years
- Full-time secretaries supporting very part-time leadership positions
- Millions of dollars of reading software never used

- Gleaming new office furniture despite a chronic shortage of desks for children
- An $18,000 annual cell phone bill (yes, for a single person)
- An increase in custodians (off budget) during widescale teacher layoffs

What all of these purchases have in common is that they happened *in the dark*. In many cases, even the so-called manager of the grant or revolving fund didn't know about these expenditures. Given that the operating budgets in most districts have been under the microscope in recent years, the other budgets are likely more fertile territory for more strategic resource allocations.

Don't Overlook Non-Operating Budgets

To effectively manage these non-operating budgets, we need to understand how they got out of control in the first place. Laws, power politics, and genuine misunderstandings contribute to the problem. Each of these special budgets typically has its own, different, mandated reporting requirements, which necessitates having its own budget. These unique reporting systems—such as combining middle and high school spending, or separating all dollars spent on support for students with early childhood needs—lead to a different chart of accounts for each budget. This means that if Mary is a speech therapist paid for by the operating budget, she and her salary are listed in the speech therapy line, but if Nancy does the same work but is paid by the IDEA grant, she is listed in a different budget as certified staff, and her salary includes health and retirement costs (unlike operating-budget Mary, who has only her base salary listed). Finally, if Joan, who is also a speech therapist, is funded through an integrated kindergarten revolving account, she is listed as integrated staff. To be clear, they all do the same job but are recorded differently. My CFO would know only that Mary is a speech therapist, and couldn't know that the two other speech therapists were hidden in other budgets.

The solution to this mandated confusion is simple, as shown in table 9.1. Each person and expense in a non-operating budget should be given

Table 9.1

Combining funding sources and staff for greater effectiveness and cost-effectiveness

Linking grants and other funding sources to the operating budget

Employee	Funding source (budget)	Line item	$	Linkage to operating budget	$
Mary	Operating budget	Speech therapy	$60,000	Speech therapy	$60,000
Nancy	IDEA grant	Speech therapy	$80,000	Speech therapy	$60,000
				Health insurance	$15,000
				Pension	$5,000
Joan	Kindergarten revolving fund	Integrated staff	$60,000	Speech therapy	$60,000

Summary based on traditional line items

Speech therapy	$140,000
Integrated staff	$60,000
Total	$200,000

Summary based on linked line items

Speech therapy	$180,000
Health insurance	$15,000
Pension	$5,000
Total	$200,000

two line-item designations: one to meet the specific needs of the grant or revolving account, and a second that maps to the operating budget. For example, Nancy would be designated as both "certified elementary" and "speech and language therapist." Moreover, Mary's benefits would be split out from her salary for the operating budget. This adds a little work for the business office, but it is the only way to effectively manage all the resources in a district.

Consolidate Funding and Departments

Beyond legal reporting requirements, turf politics contribute to the murkiness of the non-operating budgets. De facto, each budget has an unofficial owner. The special education director owns her piece, the head of food service might own the school lunch revolving account, the Title I coordinator or the head of federal grants owns Title I, and so on. The designation "owner" is, of course, unofficial, but accurate. Because each of these funds and funding sources requires someone to submit documents and manage something, it typically has a staff person assigned to oversee the reporting efforts. Assigned as a clerical, accounting, or compliance role, this person in time often grows to think of the money as his own, hence my unofficial title of "owner." Having a source of funds under your personal control and free of public scrutiny brings a great deal of power to the owners. Often, Title I, for example, will have lots of clerical support that can be loaned out to other less fortunate departments, or city-funded (but charged back to the school district) maintenance staff can be a place to transfer problematic Department of Public Works employees.

The walls that funding owners erect are high and often topped with barbed wire. One district CFO, faced with laying off hundreds of teachers, confided that the school custodial and maintenance budget had phantom staff: it listed about one hundred employees but only had closer to eighty-five real people on the payroll. The excess was "just in case" money. The CFO also told me that $2 million of federal funds was targeted for "gifts for friends," funding pet projects for supporters of a very polarizing grant owner. Sick to her stomach, the CFO produced the layoff list, without addressing any of these seemingly wasteful decisions. I asked, "Given the severity of the challenge, why not redeploy the money from the areas she had identified?" Angry and shaking, she told me it's not her place to go sticking her nose in other people's business. Mind you, she was the district's *chief financial officer.* I pushed, and said she owed it to the kids. She pushed back, saying, "They would hate me, and crush me; I would have to leave the district. I'll quit first, before you can make me take away their money."

As superintendent, I asked to see the budgets for every grant, revolving fund, off-budget account, etc. The reaction was stunned silence. When the owners realized I wasn't going to budge, the silence dissipated. "Why? You can't! It's illegal!" they shouted. Begrudgingly, they turned in nearly meaningless reports. I saw line items like $200,000 for professional development, with no indication of what topic the PD was on or how the money would be spent, and $150,000 earmarked for clerical but specifying no names or hours, let alone cost per hour. It took over six months of active digging to tease out how nearly 15 percent of our district's budget was being spent.

I did learn much quicker that these owners were popular, powerful, and the people to go to in order to fund efforts that weren't supported by the operating budget. When I heard of staff attending conferences or buying materials that didn't align with district goals (and therefore were not funded by the operating budget), I was regularly told, "Don't worry; Peg (not her real name) is paying for it." Not Title I, mind you, but Peg. It was her money, not the district's.

The power of funding sources driving program design is so strong that, in many districts, a reading teacher who is paid via Title I funds is actually listed in the school directory as the Title I teacher, not with the other reading teachers in the building. When early release time rolls around, that teacher will attend Title I professional development rather than reading PD, and the Title I office is even likely to throw a separate birthday celebration for the teacher.

Simply knowing where the money is and how it's being spent isn't enough to take control of spending. Each of these funding streams has a zillion rules, limitations, maintenance-of-effort requirements, supplement-not-suppliant conditions, and allowable uses. Many owners intentionally or unintentionally use this complexity to keep the superintendent, school board, or others out of their business. Additionally, for grant owners, noncompliance can be a career-ending event. This encourages owners to create separate programs, separate staff, and silos to ensure that their funds aren't accidentally used inappropriately. This is safe but inefficient. Elementary reading is a common Babel-like effort by owners working in silos and playing it safe. Many districts have:

- A handful of reading teachers funded by the operating budget working with general education students
- A brigade of special education teachers funded by IDEA grants working with special education students
- Two armies of noncertified tutors funded by Title I working with low-income students
- Reading intervention software paid for by Title III for ELL students
- Professional development in teaching vocabulary in the regular classroom paid for by Title II funds
- Reading books in the classroom paid for by the Teaching US History grant
- Reading coaches in some schools supervised by the School Improvement Grant owner

A single student might be served by four or five different people and programs in the same week, and principals will rightly claim that they don't have enough reading teachers or classroom reading books. The staff and funds are actually there, but they are split, splintered, and siloed. In detailed studies of ten districts from across the country, I have found a common burning desire to increase support for elementary reading by leaps and bounds. Regrettably, all the districts lacked the funds to buy the needed materials, hire the reading intervention teachers, and provide the desired staff training. They had scoured the budget and come up very short. Unfortunately for a lot of struggling readers, these districts looked only at their operating budgets. When I looked under the hood in all the other budgets, they discovered that they already spent three to five times as much as needed, but the money was spread among various funds, efforts, and staff.

In my district, for example, we pooled funds from nearly a dozen sources to implement an intensive, effective reading program. We hired a lot of reading teachers, coaches, and data experts; added materials; and provided weeks of training, all without adding a single new dollar. The results speak for themselves:

- Prior to the reform effort, the district estimated that only 10 percent of struggling elementary readers who started the school year below grade level reached grade level by year's end. After the reform efforts, over 65 percent of struggling readers became proficient readers during the school year.
- Overall, in grades K–5, the number of struggling readers declined by 68 percent, with 92.5 percent of students reading at grade level.

This success was possible because we changed our budgeting system. The CFO and superintendent became the owner of every dollar in the district, not just of the operating budget. We created one unified program, staff, and leadership team. This scared the former grant owners—and the CFO, for that matter. The accounting got complicated in the same proportion as the programs got unified. A single teacher might get paid from three sources: operating budget for periods 1, 2, and 3; Title I for half of periods 4 and 5, based on the proportion of students below the poverty line; and proportionately from IDEA, based on the percentage of special education students served. The employee got one paycheck, but was reported across three budgets. Most importantly, the students got one unified reading program. The same concept of combining funding sources bought our materials. ELL and US History grants helped supply leveled classroom libraries that tightly integrated into our core reading program. This coordination is only possible if fund management is centralized and the accounting allocated piecemeal. This is the reverse of the status quo in many districts, where the programs are separate to accommodate simple accounting. Figure 9.1 visually depicts our integrated approach to funding the reading program.

Districts that take an integrated approach to budgeting actually have budgets that look different. The standard budget is just the operating budget document. It lists line items, full-time equivalents (FTE), dollars, and maybe some comparisons to prior years.

Figure 9.1

Integrating funding sources to create unified programs

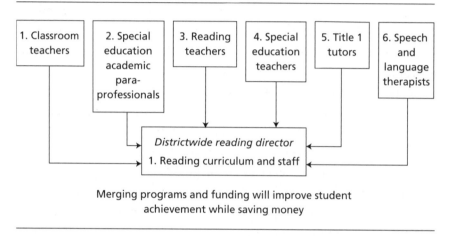

Merging programs and funding will improve student
achievement while saving money

The consolidated budget has two differences. The revenue section lists on a separate row every single source of funds, including off-budget transfers from the city or town, grants, fees, etc. The second difference is that the budget has a lot more columns. Each funding source has its own column. The district's fifty reading teachers, for example, would be on a single line, but ten may be listed in the operating budget column, fifteen in the IDEA column, twelve under Title I, and the remaining thirteen as a transfer from the integrated preschool tuition account. One program, multiple funding sources, and an easy rollup, so when a superintendent asks how many reading teachers we have, the answer is a quick fifty, not ten.

Having one budget is better than many, but it's important that it be accurate and useful, not just consolidated. Unfortunately, many school district budgets aren't great decision-making tools. Organizational structure and culture, not people, are the root cause.

Rethink Your Budget Design

Most business offices are isolated from the schools they serve, and most CFOs were never teachers or principals. At the same time, most principals and administrators don't use budgets every month. This division can lead to the garbage in, garbage out problem. The people in the business office who code many of the expenses don't actually know what the expense is used for or what line items would be most meaningful. This is especially true for new ventures. One district started in-house severe-needs special education programs, but listed all the expenses as "other," thus obscuring important information. At the same time, the people who *do* know that this is a silly classification don't care, because they aren't tasked with managing the budget. Why fix someone else's problem?

This is not a small problem. Without good, detailed budget information, even the best of leaders can't manage dollars wisely. School transportation is a powerful example. In some districts, busing can account for 3 to 7 percent of total spending—tens of millions of dollars in large districts and $1 million in a midsized district. The typical district budget might look like this:

- Bus drivers listed in the salary lines
- Equipment maintenance in the maintenance section
- Bus monitors listed in the special education paraprofessional line item
- Gas in the utilities line, buried in with oil for the heating system

Together, these lines total less than 20 percent of the full cost to transport students in the district, because this district subcontracts much of its general education and special education transportation. The majority of the costs will be listed, but not separately, in the purchased services line item, which might also include lawyers, elevator repairs, and computer network support.

Here's what could be hidden from view in a budget like this:

- The number of buses for general education increased despite no increase in the number of students.
- The average cost of transporting a special education student rose 15 percent over two years.
- IEP teams are now twice as likely to require a special education bus monitor as they were three years ago.

- The decision to provide more athletic transportation, budgeted at a nominal incremental cost, actually raised costs by ten times more than planned because additional buses and drivers were needed due to changes to the bell schedule at some schools.

The single line item, "purchased services," will get passed over during many budget reviews, but detailed information gets studied—what gets measured gets managed. A more detailed transportation budget design would have exposed all these issues, as depicted in table 9.2.

Budget Using Actuals

There is another important, but technical, consideration that helps make budget documents better. Returning to that basic question I asked my CFO—"How much do we spend on teachers?"—even if he rolled up teachers funded from the multitude of budgets, he would still be wrong. He would have told me only what we *planned* to spend, not what we *actually* spent. Most districts in my experience manage from their budget figures, not actual expenditures. Worse yet, some districts simply roll over last year's estimate to the next year, without ever updating based on actuals. Again, this is a systems problem.

The 2012–2013 budget for the school year starting September 2012 is crafted in January, just a few months into the 2011–2012 school year. At this point in time, no one knows what actual spending will be for 2011–2012. The next year's budget is approved in the spring, again, before this year's actual costs are known. When June 30 rolls around and final spending is tallied, everyone is tired of budgets and starting to plan for 2013–2014! In the private-sector setting, the budget would be reconfirmed/adjusted once year-end actuals are known. Equally important, future budgets would build from those actuals, not from prior budget figures.

This process is the most common reason districts overspend. It's easy. Let's say we budget for twenty-five first-grade teachers, for a total cost of $1.5 million, at an average salary of $60,000. The number of teachers isn't likely to change, but spending might. What if five veteran staff members are replaced with younger teachers, each earning $20,000

Table 9.2

Sample transportation budget detail

Line item	Number of buses	Number of runs	Number of children	Drivers	Monitors	Equipment	Gas	Contracted	Total
In-district general education transportation—district staff	xx	xx	xx	$$$	$$$	$$$	$$$		$$$
In-district general education transportation—subcontracted	xx	xx	xx		$$$			$$$	$$$
Subtotal general education transportation	xx	xx	xx	$$$	$$$	$$$	$$$	$$$	$$$
In-district special education transportation—district staff	xx	xx	xx	$$$	$$$	$$$	$$$		$$$
In-district special education transportation—subcontracted	xx	xx	xx		$$$			$$$	$$$
Out-of-district special education transportation—district staff	xx	xx	xx	$$$	$$$	$$$	$$$		$$$
Out-of-district special education transportation—subcontracted	xx	xx	xx		$$$			$$$	$$$
Subtotal for special education transportation	xx	xx	xx	$$$	$$$	$$$	$$$	$$$	$$$
Grand total for transportation	xx	xx	xx	$$$	$$$	$$$	$$$	$$$	$$$

less? This creates a surplus of $100,000, despite no change in staffing levels. The same process can work in the other direction as well. In some districts, as enrollment changes over the summer, maybe two new first-grade teachers are added, but again, their budgets don't change to reflect this.

Sometimes budget numbers are just plain wrong. In one district, heat and electricity line items went up by 2 percent each year, and maintenance costs were estimated to be flat. Year after year, no one needed to spend time managing these areas, because the budget said they were under control. The budget lied.

Utilities costs actually roller-coastered up and down 20 percent year to year, and maintenance had grown 50 percent. When asked why the budget didn't reflect reality, the CFO explained that the prior CFO made the rule about utilities, and no one likes to spend money on maintenance, so the increases were placed in other lines. Once it knew the truth, the district upgraded to energy-efficient lights, switched some schools to natural gas, and put maintenance contracts out to bid. In short, it managed these expenses.

If you're surprised that the budget wasn't 100 percent accurate, you have never run a school district that doesn't have a reserve account. In some states, school districts are barred by law from having the equivalent of a savings account, despite the fact that budgets are set eighteen months in advance. How do you plan for unforeseen expenses, such as new special education costs? Some pad certain line items or don't plan to spend everything in the off-budget accounts. This makes factual budget analysis difficult and prudent expense management hard. A simple fix, which doesn't require state laws to change, would be to create a line item for unplanned expenses equal to, say, 1 percent of the budget.

Change the Incentive System

The one system, however, that is the most broken in public school finance may also be the hardest to fix because it can't be repaired with a spreadsheet, a computer, or a law. The incentive system is all wrong. An unstated premise throughout this book has been that we want to do the best for kids despite the tight financial times. This is true, but just partially true in most school districts I have worked with and in. There are many other incentives that counterbalance the Norman Rockwell–esque "kids come first" mantra. Equally powerful forces include:

- Principals want to save the jobs of their teachers, even if enrollment has dropped in their schools.
- The head of maintenance wants to protect the custodians, even if outsourcing would save 20 percent.
- The head of math wants more math teachers and a new math curriculum, even if English achievement is struggling more.
- The head of nursing wants a lot more nurses, even if the district has typical staffing levels.

The full list could go on for pages.

The desire to save jobs and garner resources for "your team" is powerful. I'm often reminded of *Charlotte's Web* during my budget deliberations. Fern, if you remember, had a pet pig named Wilbur. One takeaway from this classic story is we can have a pet pig and still want a ham sandwich for lunch, but we want the ham from someone else's pig. The reasonable and humane desire to save friends and colleagues makes effective budget development difficult. This is human nature. Some leaders can't look past the pain of impacting their staff, even if it just means transferring a teacher to another building or sharing an art teacher between two schools. Instead, they create class lists or schedules that prevent the changes. Often, it seems that only the superintendent is looking at the entire system.

The problem of thoughtfully managing resources is compounded by what I call *budget blindness.* Just as parents have difficulty seeing that their child is the one causing the stir at the birthday party, leaders seldom can see that their staff is underscheduled or not the highest priority for student learning. Unfortunately, these very same near-sighted leaders should best be able to find more efficient and effective uses of funds. They are the closest to the action and know, really know, what everyone is doing.

The challenge is to reverse the incentives. The following sections detail a five-step approach to align the interests of principals and department leaders with the good of the whole system.

1. Share Information Widely

For example, the math department head doesn't really know that the math teachers have an average class of nineteen students, while English, science, and social studies each average twenty-one students. Confronted with this fact, the department head might find the decision to reduce math teachers more acceptable.

2. Share the Benefit, Not Just the Pain

The superintendent might be thanked (maybe) for balancing a budget and bringing equity to class size across the district by assigning teachers based on actual enrollment. It is the principal, however, who has to deliver the unpleasant message to two loyal teachers that they are being transferred to another school. Through tears, one is likely to ask, "Why didn't you fight for me?!" This is an awful conversation, and in my experience, many principals will make heroic efforts to avoid it. My principals did. They pushed back at every change to staffing in their buildings. I got tired of the fighting and made them an offer. For every dollar they cut from their budget (subject to approval), they could decide how to spend half the savings. In short order, dozens of previously "indispensable" positions were offered up in exchange for more reading teachers, social workers, and clerical support. In just a few weeks, they found great ideas that had eluded the central office over two years of searching.

3. Let Them Walk in Your Shoes

One year, I was dreading balancing the budget. Not because it was difficult or hard on kids—in fact, we had lots of reasonable options—but mostly because I was dreading the pushback. Everyone was going to hound me—as if I asked the state to reduce our funding! In frustration, I gave my top twenty people the list of possible cuts, shifts, and new investments. Each line had an idea and the associated impact in dollars. I asked them how they would balance the budget. They howled and said this is hard, too hard. I insisted they take a stab at balancing the budget. What emerged amazed and pleased me. Many wrote in new ideas, some wrote in suggestions they had opposed in the past, and all wrestled with the trade-offs.

The process was so effective in creating shared ownership and thoughtful decisions that we decided to allow the whole town to participate in the exercise. We posted a web-based tool that required the residents in town to balance the budget given a limited number of choices. Over one-third of the families in town responded with thoughtful decisions. Parents selected options the school board would never have considered, including higher fees.

4. Focus on Formulas, Not Faces

School budgets are about people—their work and their livelihoods. That makes it hard. Rules-based staffing helps depersonalize the process. If a school gets one art teacher for every twenty-five classrooms, then a school that drops five classrooms knows automatically that 0.2 FTE of an art teacher's time will be shared with another school. The principal can deliver the news as "I'm sorry, but the guidelines require twenty-five classes per art teacher" rather than, "we cut your full-time spot to balance the budget," and then have to defend why the district didn't cut the assistant principal or a classroom aide instead.

5. Create a True Team

The most powerful, effective, and efficient budget is developed when all the principals, department heads, and curriculum leaders leave their parochial team and are traded to the district team.

Fans of Patrick Lencioni's *The Five Dysfunctions of a Team* will get the reference. In this best-selling book, readers see a company's sales, marketing, engineering, production, and other departments slowly migrate from department loyalty to whole-company loyalty. The CEO asks them to put the overall company's needs above their respective departments—that is, to make the company their first team.[1]

I loved this concept, and needed my cabinet to put the district first when building a budget. In fact, I handed out over five hundred copies of the book and led an extended discussion group with my leadership team. When team members fully understood what I was asking, one principal declared, "My school is my team, and it always will be!" Saddened but undeterred, I hired an organizational expert to help us build a true team. Over two years, with Myers-Briggs, 360-degree reviews, confidential interviews, much shouting, some tears, and a few resignations, we forged a team. The result was much smarter budgets and smarter schools. The high school principal shifted resources to the growing enrollment at the elementary level, the social studies department pooled funds with reading, and our new team presented tough decisions to the public with a united front.

The one great irony was that the small investment I made in buying the book and hiring a team-building consultant was roundly criticized as not protecting the classroom or small class sizes. As I have stated often, it is not easy to build smarter budgets and get smarter schools, but it is worth the effort when you see the gains in student learning and expanded services.

Consolidate Departments

Collaboration is great, but hard to achieve. In districts across the country, I hear the same pleas: "I wish special education and general education would work more closely," or "I wish ELL, curriculum, and Title I reading tutors would all be on the same page."

If leaders are inclined to protect their turf, the fewer departments a district has, the fewer turf battles need to be fought. When I combined six reading programs, staff and funds, into a single department under a single leader, it became easy to move dollars around within the department and create a much more effective and cost-effective effort. Cross-departmental cooperation wasn't needed to get more out of limited funds. It seems it is easier to knock down walls than build bridges.

A CRAZY IDEA?

CFO as Instructional Leader

Over the last decade, the role of the school principal has evolved from building manager to instructional leader. As the theory goes, the principal has to drive effective instruction and, as a corollary, should know what good teaching looks and feels like. Why isn't the same expected from the chief financial officer?

In my experience, most district CFOs are asked to track spending, produce documents, and file reports. In hundreds of meetings across scores of districts, I have seldom found the CFO to be an active participant in strategy development or the leader in increasing the cost-effectiveness of academic efforts. In fact, CFOs don't usually attend these meetings. Who else in the district has the skills to lead an effort to raise its A-ROI?

It's funny; many CFOs tightly analyze, manage, and improve food or custodial services because these are under their domain. What about the other 95 percent of the budget?

It is different in the private sector, where CFOs are often business strategists, involved in all key decisions. The CFO can be such a broad-based, big-picture role that one can rise to be the visionary CEOs at companies like Pfizer, Burger King, Maytag, and the like. As CFO.com explains: "The reasons for this are compelling. Over the past decade, finance executives have become more involved in strategy; they have been given operations oversight; and as they have taken a broader view of the organization, they have worked intimately with the CEO. 'CFOs penetrate all facets of a business, which is critical to understanding what levers to push as the CEO,' says Frank E. Weise III, CEO of Cott Corp. and former CFO of The Campbell Soup Co."[2]

Should the district CFO know the research on class size, understand value-added growth scores, embrace early reading intervention efforts, and help the district make wise spending decisions? CFOs could be the other "minister without portfolio." Like superintendents, they could care about the entire district, not just a school (like a principal) or a department (like a curriculum leader). They could be powerful strategic partners for superintendents.

The CFO as instructional leader requires the role to become the strategy and finance quarterback, not the scorekeeper. CFOs would actively look for ways to raise achievement while lowering costs, and would most likely own the A-ROI efforts. This might require a different background and training. These CFOs might need both MBAs and teaching degrees, as well as a passion for numbers and pedagogy. Fortunately, there is an emerging pool of such people. The Broad Foundation—through its residency program, Teach For America—and high-performing charter management organizations are attracting MBAs and CPAs into the classroom and then into district leadership roles. Their training and experience is just the right combination to forge a CFO as instructional leader. The role would also be an effective training ground for future superintendents, who will be asked to raise student achievement despite declining resources.

10

Getting Started

*Given the hundreds of ideas for smarter budgets and smarter
schools, which ones are appropriate for your school system?
District strategy should dictate where to start and what to skip.*

I love a buffet. The Chinese kind is good, but the international is even
better. With gluttonous eyes, I load General Gao's chicken next to
southern fried chicken, slide them both to the edge of the plate to make
room for a taco and a bit of lasagna, and finally top everything with a
small pyramid of sushi. Buffets bring out the worst in me, and likewise,
without exercising some self-control, school districts might allow this
book's first nine chapters to become an unhealthy budget smorgasbord.
It is a mistake to select your favorite budget balancing idea, use it to
close next year's funding shortfall, and declare success. A good solution
for one district may be inappropriate or even harmful for its neighbor.
District strategy and local context should drive which "do more with
less" options are worth pursuing.

Create a Clear Theory of Action

District *strategy* shouldn't be confused with a district's strategic *plan*. The plan can be a document that lists specific activities to be done by a certain date with specific targets for achievement. While helpful, the strategic plan often presupposes the current structures and approaches—some of which might be changed in an effort to bend the cost curve. The district's strategy (also called a *theory of action*), on the other hand, shouldn't change as a result of budgeting; in fact, it should drive budgeting. A theory of action is the logic behind how the district hopes to improve. It is often structured as a series of because-if-then statements. A few common examples are:

- **Great teachers:** *Because* teacher effectiveness is the most important driver of student success, *if* we recruit, hire, and retain top teachers, *then* the quality of instruction will improve and student achievement will rise.
- **Empowerment:** *Because* decisions made closest to the student can best be tailored to individual needs, *if* we empower principals to have autonomy and control of their budgets, subject to accountability, *then* resources will be more wisely spent and *then* supports and approaches will be more customized, which will raise student achievement.

There are many effective theories of action, but as these two examples suggest, they can vary greatly from one another. Different strategies will favor different approaches to rethinking school budgets. The "great teachers" theory of action might suggest outsourcing human resources to ensure an efficient, effective system of soliciting and processing applicants. It could also encourage outsourcing noncore instruction so that principals would have fewer staff members to manage and could focus their efforts on classroom and core-subject teachers. A more mundane "great teachers" budget implication might warrant detailed staffing to enrollment and/or larger class sizes, to fund higher starting pay to attract and retain top talent.

In contrast, the "empowerment" route doesn't require careful central office staffing to enrollment or even the controversial class size debate. These decisions are made by each principal. The district and principals would, however, benefit from consolidated budgets that show operating funds, Title I, IDEA, and all other dollars in an easy-to-read, easy-to-understand way. A district pursuing this theory of action might also benefit from substituting noncertified staff in library, art, music, PE, or nursing to free up even more funds to be redeployed by each principal. Ensuring that fully loaded costs are being managed, including benefits, is also important in this model.

Matching resource strategies to district strategy takes discipline, but the logic isn't hard to follow. The task is harder if the district doesn't have a clear theory of action. Many superintendents and school boards have shared, "We really don't have a theory of action; we just manage based on experience, the limit of our resources, and what's best for kids." Sometimes, these districts pull out the concentric circles diagram from last year's budget discussion, which shows core subjects in the center, noncore subjects in the next ring, administration in the third, and everything else in the fourth.

In my experience, nearly all districts have a very well-developed theory of action, but it's often unstated. A look at their budgets reveals the implicit priorities and strategies; for example:

- Budgets that maintain small classes state unambiguously a belief that small class size raises student achievement.
- Districts that have cut reading teachers, department heads, data analysts, coaches, mentors, building-based secretaries, or central office administrators imply that "protecting the classroom" will raise achievement, even if each classroom teacher is provided less support.
- Districts that have reduced art, PE, or music believe that class size limits for core classes should be the same as for noncore subjects.

Thoughtful discussion, a careful review of past spending decisions, and a detailed read of the current budget can help bring a hidden theory of action into daylight. As budgets tighten, all districts need an explicit strategy, and because-if-then logic to drive how to allocate limited resources.

Don't Overlook Context

Having a theory of action, however, isn't enough. Napoleon had a great plan to march on Russia, a plan that worked well against the nations of continental Europe. Unfortunately, Moscow is farther away and a lot colder. A plan that had been successful elsewhere failed dramatically due to differing context. For school districts, context is mostly defined by culture, politics, and contracts.

Culture

Perhaps the most critical aspect of culture is the sense of urgency—both achievement urgency and financial urgency. I have visited schools where less than 25 percent of students are proficient, but parents, teachers, and principals are basically OK. They want improvement and take comfort from the fact that plans are in place. I have also visited blue-ribbon schools hell-bent on raising already high results to the next level. Test scores often do not correlate to the desire to try new ideas or to stomach hard decisions. Financial urgency seems to be following the same less-than-data-driven pattern. I have witnessed panic at budget cuts that drop spending down to $22,000 a student, and total calm at reductions yielding only $8,000 a student. Urgency is a belief, not a statement of fact. Districts with urgency—whether achievement-based or financial—can embrace sweeping changes. Many a reform-minded superintendent has swept into town, looked around, and declared a state of emergency. Before revamping your resource allocation plans, gauge who else shares a dire assessment of the situation.

Community values also drive school culture. Some communities embrace more of a free-market leaning; in others, union pride runs deep. Outsourcing and subcontracting can be dead on arrival in one district and embraced as wise stewardship in another.

Politics

Understanding the context of a district can help with navigating the politics. Politics, in large part, marks the boundaries between doable and job-threatening. Unlike presidential politics, where 51 percent of the vote carries the day, school budget politics isn't about simple majorities. A small group, when greatly impacted by changes in funding, can be a powerful force. I have seen this firsthand. The worst budget decision I ever made was to reduce the work hours of crossing guards. Before images of cruel, heartless, axe-wielding bureaucrats rush to mind, consider these facts:

- Six of seven school board members listed trimming the crossing guards as a top priority.
- The chief of police, the head safety officer in town, had long wanted to bring sanity to an out-of-control situation and strongly supported the plan.
- Two pro bono traffic consultants helped to design the reorganization.
- One-third of the crossing guards crossed *no* children walking to school without their parent. Some crossed *no* children at all!
- The crossing guards were paid to work 50 percent more hours than kids actually walked to or from school.
- The most dangerous intersection had no coverage because the crossing guards thought it was unsafe for them!

Logically, this was a prudent way to save $100,000 and keep two reading teachers that might otherwise be cut. Logic, however, has nothing to do with politics. These nice little old ladies had been welcoming children and their parents for twenty-five years. They were beloved by many and a symbol of the Irish Catholic, working-class roots of the community, a group whose hold on power was slipping due to "new arrivals" in town. The seemingly prudent decision to trim the hours of the crossing guards erupted into a three-year fight that wouldn't end, even when the decision was reversed. School board meetings, town meetings, and PTO meetings regularly had thirty angry ladies in orange vests screaming, "Children will die!" Before the dust settled, the uproar led to the ousting of reform-minded school board members, grievances, a civil service complaint, and a crossing guard union. It also undermined my ability to drive other budget reforms as the board and other district leaders became gun-shy.

The story highlights the essence of budget politics. The gains help many a little bit, but hurt a few a whole lot. The injured are highly motivated. Picking battles carefully is a key component to surviving and thriving in tight times.

Teacher demographics and changes in student enrollment also impact a district's political climate. I have watched many districts try to shift reading support from paraprofessionals to certified reading teachers, or to reduce special education teachers to add response to intervention (RTI) staff or behaviorists. In systems with high staff turnover, each new hire is a pain-free chance to move resources. The plans can be phased in as staff members leave and new roles are hired in their stead. For districts with rising enrollments, the opening of new schools is also an opportunity to staff differently without impacting existing staff. Often, moving or replacing untenured teachers also requires little political capital. These same changes impacting a tenth as many veteran staff members can erupt into a political firestorm.

Contracts

Union contracts also shape the context of many districts. Few of the ideas presented in these pages require negotiating changes to union agreements, while some could benefit from relaxing contractual limitations. Labor agreements set the wage rates, and when and if union wages and benefits exceed market wages, the financial gains from outsourcing and subcontracting increase. Beyond dollars and cents, union "bumping" rules for reduction in force can greatly complicate strategically shifting resources. One of the unintended consequences of my staffing to enrollment effort was moving veteran staff members who didn't have full-time teaching loads, but did have a slew of old certifications, into roles where learning would suffer. Based on thoughtful staffing guidelines, a drama teacher would be bumped into the English department, a librarian would be shifted into a social studies class, and a non-Spanish-speaking social studies teacher, who was certified (somehow), would have taught Spanish 1 and 2. Despite their certifications, none were qualified. In these cases, saving money was going to lower achievement, and thus was not a bargain worth making.

On the flip side, a careful reading of the contract can reveal more latitude than expected. I have seen a number of districts discover that they had more authority to reassign staff midyear as student needs changed, share staff between buildings, outsource, trade down, or change job descriptions.

Every district has its unique context, but there are two universal ideas for successfully rethinking the effectiveness and cost-effectiveness of limited funds. The first is to focus on the gain, not the loss, and the second is to never to try this alone.

Emphasize the Gains

Cutting the budget is never fun, and seldom welcomed. Helping kids is. New ideas and approaches that simultaneously raise achievement and reduce costs are easier to enact than lose-lose reductions only.

One superintendent friend learned this lesson the hard way. The district had unusually high numbers of special education paraprofessionals, and she crafted a plan to trim just a few (less than 5 percent). Best of all, through better scheduling, not a minute of support would be removed from a single student. Better scheduling would help close a budget shortfall. Like the story of the pharaoh of Egypt, though, ten plagues rained from an angry hand. Parents were upset, principals hinted that kids would suffer, teachers panicked, the press was bad, and the plan was dropped. Move ahead a year later, and add a new intensive reading program with intervention from skilled reading teachers. The plan eliminated 25 percent of the paraprofessionals, shifted resources to certified staff, and lowered the operating budget. No screams. Just praise and smooth sailing. Despite impacting five times as many adults, the plan and the pain were tolerable because the gain was obvious and welcomed.

The concept of bundling more for kids while spending less can be applied widely. This is putting the "more" back into "more for less." For example, a district wanting to embrace online hybrid courses in math or science could also greatly expand what electives are offered through self-directed distance learning at the same time. If class sizes for non-core subjects are going to increase, some of the savings could be used for expanded opportunities for an art show, more drama productions, or band concerts. If just 10 percent if the savings is redeployed to provide targeted embellishments to the district's offerings, change will be easier to accept. Often, the parents most upset at the change will be the same ones most likely to have their children take advantage of add-ons.

Find Strength in Numbers

Finally, anyone charged with managing school budgets should keep in mind the lesson many learned in summer camp or at the YMCA—never swim alone. Superintendents or school boards often feel that managing the budget is their responsibility, and that shielding others from this unpleasant task is part of the job description. Neither the lone wolf nor the martyr makes the best resource allocation decisions. Managing a district budget is as much political as it is technical, and buy-in matters as much as bright ideas.

Working closely with teachers, principals, municipal leaders, union heads, parents, and the community can help ease acceptance of changes to the budget. Since people tend to look at issues with a lens colored by their personal experiences and interest, it is easier to find a common ground through common information. The ideas from chapter 9 will help. Creating a common understanding of the reality, trade-offs, and student benefits can help build coalitions. It worked for me in the case of librarians, but not with the crossing guards, which brings me to my final point.

Budget cuts, new technology, different staffing models, and larger class sizes are coming to virtually every district in the United States. The

Great Recession, drops in state tax revenues, and escalating costs make this inevitable. The only question is whether these financial forces will decimate the education our children receive, or transform it. If we keep student needs at the fore and embrace new ideas, approaches, systems, and technology, the future needn't be bleak. It won't be easy, and many will mourn the changes, but the financial crisis can accelerate the transition to a different—but better—way of ensuring that all children are ready for success in work, life, and society. I hope these ideas help lead the way. Good luck!

Notes

Chapter 2

1. Arne Duncan, "The New Normal: Doing More with Less" (speech, American Enterprise Institute, Washington, DC, November 17, 2010).
2. Karen Rutzick, "On Call: Without a nurse at each school, teachers struggle to provide medical care," *Education Week Teacher*, April 20, 2007.

Chapter 3

1. Edward Moscovitch, *School Funding Reality: A Bargain Not Kept* (Boston: Massachusetts Business Alliance for Education [MBAE], 2010).
2. Towers Watson/National Business Group on Health, "The Road Ahead: Shaping Health Care Strategy in a Post-Reform Environment," 16th Annual Employer Survey on Purchasing Value in Health Care, http://www.towerswatson.com/assets/pdf/3946/TowersWatson-NBGH-2011-NA-2010-18560.pdf.
3. Wisconsin Association of School Boards, "10–11 Health Insurance Data," WASB School District Settlement Database, http://www.wasb.org/websites/employment_law_hr_services/File/health_insurance_cost_contribution_comparisons/1011_teacher_health_insurance_data.pdf.
4. Josh Barro and Stuart Buck, "Underfunded Teacher Pension Plans: It's Worse Than You Think," *Civic Report 61*, Manhattan Institute for Policy Research (2010).
5. Robert M. Costrell, "Oh, to Be a Teacher in Wisconsin," *Wall Street Journal*, February 25, 2011.

Chapter 4

1. Grover J. ("Russ") Whitehurst and Matthew M. Chingos, *Class Size: What Research Says and What It Means for State Policy* (Washington, DC: Brown Center on Education Policy at Brookings, 2011).
2. Arne Duncan, "The New Normal: Doing More with Less" (speech, American Enterprise Institute, Washington, DC, November 17, 2010).

Chapter 5

1. Erik W. Robelen, "NAEP Results Show Math Gains, But 4th Grade Reading Still Flat," *Education Week*, November 9, 2011: 5–6.
2. Rennie Center for Education Research & Policy, *Seeking Effective Policies and Practices for Students with Special Needs* (Cambridge, MA: Rennie Center for Education Research & Policy, 2009).
3. Ibid.

4. Sarah D. Sparks, "Study: Third Grade Reading Predicts Later High School Graduation." *Inside School Research* (blog), *Education Week*, April 8, 2011, http://blogs.edweek.org/edweek/inside-school-research/2011/04/the_disquieting_side_effect_of.html.

5. National Center for Education Statistics, "Table 3. Number of staff for public schools, by category and state jurisdiction: School year 2006–07," http://nces.ed.gov/ccd/tables/2009305_03.asp.

6. Rennie Center, *Seeking Effective Policies and Practices*.

7. Ibid.

Chapter 6

1. Rick Hess, "Getting Serious About Bang for the Buck," *Rick Hess Straight Up* (blog), *Education Week*, January 25, 2011, http://blogs.edweek.org/edweek/rick_hess_straight_up/2011/01/getting_serious_about_bang_for_the_buck.html.

2. US Department of Education, Office of Special Education Programs, Data Accountability Center, https://www.ideadata.org/default.asp.

3. Barack Obama, "New Hampshire Primary Speech," January 8, 2008, transcript, *New York Times*, http://www.nytimes.com/2008/01/08/us/politics/08text-obama.html?pagewanted=all.

4. National Center for Education Statistics, "Table 3. Number of staff for public schools, by category and state jurisdiction: School year 2006–07," http://nces.ed.gov/ccd/tables/2009305_03.asp.

5. Thomas Hehir, "Eliminating Ableism in Education," *Harvard Educational Review* (Cambridge, MA: President and Fellows of Harvard College, 2002).

Chapter 7

1. Claudia Wallis, "How to Bring Our Schools Out of the 20th Century," *Time*, December 10, 2006.

2. David Nagel, "Education IT Spending, Fueled by Telecom, To Top $56 Billion by 2012," *Campus Technology*, September 19, 2008, http://campustechnology.com/Articles/2008/09/Education-IT-Spending-Fueled-by-Telecom-To-Top-56-Billion-by-2012.aspx.

3. Matt Ritchel, "In Classroom of Future, Stagnant Scores," *The New York Times*, September 3, 2011.

4. Doug Johnson, "Stretching Your Technology Dollar," *Educational Leadership*, vol. 69, no. 4 (December 2011–January 2012): 30–33.

5. Ibid.

6. Jeffrey R. Young, "Absent Students Want to Attend Traditional Classes via Webcam," *The Chronicle of Higher Education*, November 25, 2011.

7. Bill Gates, "Bill Gates Outlines Vision for Using Technology To Create More Effective and Efficient Schools" (speech, American Association of School Administrators Annual Conference, New Orleans, February 22, 1999, http://www.microsoft.com/presspass/exec/billg/speeches/1999/02-22aasa.aspx).

8. "Home Computer Access and Internet Use," last modified June 2010, http://www.childtrendsdatabank.org/?q=node/298.

9. Amanda Lenhart, Kristen Purcell, Aaron Smith, and Kathryn Zickuhr, *Social Media & Mobile Internet Use Among Teens and Young Adults*, Pew Internet & American Life Project (Washington, DC: Pew Research Center, 2010).

Chapter 8

1. Katy Murphy, "Angry Crowd Demands the Oakland School board Keep Schools Open," *MercuryNews.com*, October 27, 2011, http://www.mercurynews.com/breaking-news/ci_19207968.
2. Massachusetts School Building Authority, *2006–2007 Annual Report* (Boston: Massachusetts School Building Authority, 2007).

Chapter 9

1. Patrick Lencioni, *The Five Dysfunctions of a Team: A Leadership Fable* (San Francisco: Jossey-Bass, 2002).
2. Stephen Barr, "CFOs-Turned-CEOs: The View from the Other Side of the Desk," September 27, 2001, http://www.cfo.com/article.cfm/3000693?f=search.

About the Author

Nathan Levenson began his career in the private sector, starting as a strategic planning management consultant, the owner of a midsized manufacturer of highly engineered machinery, and a turnaround consultant helping struggling firms. A passion for public education led to a career switch that included six years as a school board member, an assistant superintendent for curriculum and instruction in Harvard, Massachusetts, and superintendent of the Arlington (Massachusetts) Public Schools.

Nathan's leadership led to widescale changes in academic programs by accelerating the move to standards-based education and teacher-developed common formative assessments in reading, math, writing, and social studies.

He helped create and champion an intensive reading program that reduced the number of students reading below grade level by 68 percent and revamped special education services, leading to a 24 percentage-point improvement in academic achievement in English and math. The Rennie Center for Education Research and Policy identified Arlington High as a best-practice school for raising achievement of students with special needs by more than nearly all other schools in the state, a two-thirds reduction in the achievement gap.

By redesigning its budgeting, custodial, financial accounting, and leadership structure, the Arlington district created significant savings while providing higher service levels in all areas that were affected. Savings were shifted to academic programs that helped students directly. As a strong believer in the importance of developing staff, Nathan implemented a new system for hiring teachers and created teamwork between administrators and teams of teachers, despite an environment that had previously prized isolation and turf conflict.

Nathan is currently managing director of the District Management Council in Boston, an organization committed to helping public school districts raise student achievement, improve operations, and control costs—all at the same time. Through the organization's network of leading districts and extensive consulting, Nathan has studied in depth more than fifty districts from coast to coast, with each district ranging from a few thousand students to hundreds of thousands. His work has also included conducting primary research in the areas of strategic planning, budgeting, and special education.

Nathan's work has been profiled in the *District Management Journal*, in the Rennie Center for Education Research and Policy's *Best Practices in Special Education* report, and in Frederick M. Hess and Eric Osberg's *Stretching the School Dollar: How Schools and Districts Can Save Money While Serving Students Best* (Harvard Education Press). He has written numerous articles on the topic of doing more with less in public schools.

Nathan received a BA from Dartmouth College and an MBA with distinction from Harvard Business School, and is a graduate of the Broad Foundation Urban Superintendents Academy.

Index